Tribute to Paula Ramsey
"Mom"

Paula Ramsey, founder & owner of "A Lady's Day Out" has gone to be with her sweet savior. On August 22, 2000 she lost her battle with cancer. Mom's life was an example for many. We can all be assured her rewards were great and that the Father welcomed her home with open arms and a big "Thank you" for a life spent glorifying Him and bringing many into the Kingdom.

"A Lady's Day Out" was Mom's vision. As with most things in her life, she was willing to share this with me. We traveled from one exciting town to the next—finding treasures and experiencing so much together for more than 10 years. I was blessed to have shared these times with my mom and hold them dear in the quiet places of my heart.

The loss of my best friend, business partner and mother is great, and the pain is deep. Our family has lost our "rock," but our faith in the Lord is strong, and we take comfort in knowing we will someday join her again in heaven.

I will miss our adventures together, but I am thankful for the times we shared, and I feel blessed to have had a mom that others could only dream of. I have always been and will continue to be proud of my mother for her love of the Lord, her right choices, her ability to lead by example and the contributions she made here on earth. Mom had an unconditional love for all of her children, and as her daughter, I will miss that attribute the most.

We will continue to publish "A Lady's Day Out" books and see her vision through. A percentage of all book sales will go to charity in Mom's memory. Thank you for celebrating her memory with us. Each time you pick up this book or any of our others, we hope you think of Mom and her inspiration—Jesus Christ.

Jennifer "Jenni" Ramsey

Abigaile's Treehouse   *(See related story page 191 and on front cover.)*

Angel's Nest *(See related story page 89.)*

Granbury, Texas *(See related stories beginning on page 8.)*

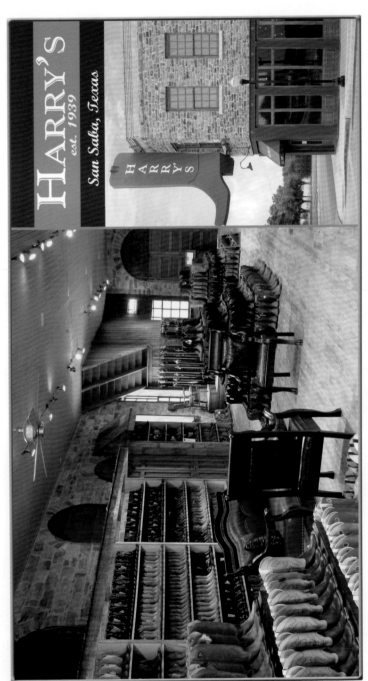

Harry's *(See related story page 259.)*

Clark Gardens *(See related story page 86.)*

Henderson, Texas *(See related stories beginning page 115.)*

B.J. Taylor & Co. *(See related story page 126.)*

Bermuda Gold & Silver *(See related story page 69.)*

Doss Heritage and Culture Center *(See related story page 87.)*

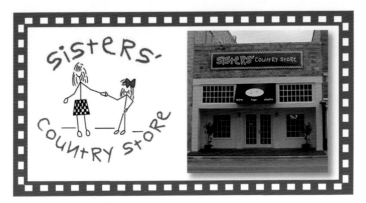

Sisters' *(See related story page 260.)*

Bella Rosa *(See related story page 26.)*

Pamela & Co. *(See related story page 34.)*

Kilgore, Texas *(See related stories beginning page 136.)*

The Clary House *(See related story page 191.)*

Street Musicians, Mineola, Texas
(See related stories beginning page 156.)

Inn on the Creek
(See related story page 224.)

Calvert Victorian Tea & Gala
(See related stories beginning page 201.)

Jordan's Plant Farm
(See related story page 128.)

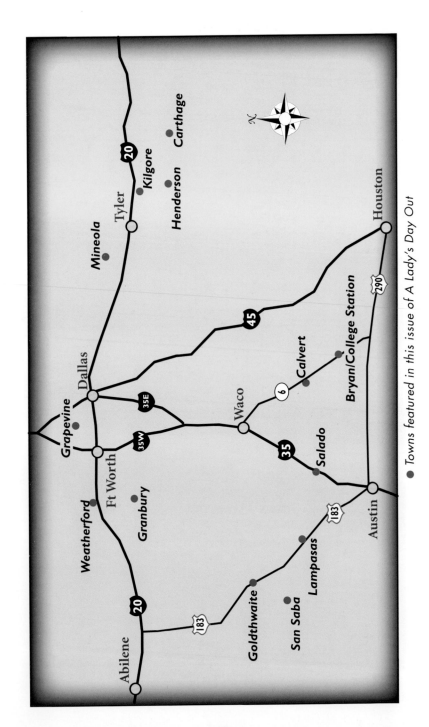

● Towns featured in this issue of *A Lady's Day Out*

Available Titles

After enjoying this book, we are sure you will also love our other books:

"A LADY'S DAY OUT IN THE TEXAS HILL COUNTRY, VOL. III"

Spiced with local history and Heritage; this book is our latest edition for the Texas Hill Country. Featuring the best Bed & Breakfast, Inns, Cottages, Art Galleries, Antiques, Tea Rooms, Restaurants, Unique Boutiques, Specialty Shops, Attractions and Entertainment the Hill Country has to offer. Find out why the Texas Hill Country is a favorite destination for all. Plan your trip by using this book and you'll be sure to guide yourself to the best and most unique towns and shops the Hill Country has to offer. Featuring the wonderful towns of Brownwood, Buchanan Dam, Burnet, Comfort, Comanche, Early, Fredericksburg, Hamilton, Johnson City, Kerrville, Kingsland, Llano, Marble Falls, Mason and Wimberley. Hard Cover—*302 Pages - $19.95*

"A LADY'S DAY OUT IN SAN ANTONIO AND SURROUNDING AREAS, VOL. II"

San Antonio is brought to life on the sizzling pages of this book. Let us acquaint you with this enchanting city full of great shopping, fabulous cuisine, a vibrant Riverwalk and deep tradition. Within just a few minutes from the city, we have also included the destinations of Alamo Heights, Bandera, Boerne, Bracken, Bulverde, Canyon Lake, Gruene, Monte Vista, New Braunfels, Olmos Park and Terrell Hills. Hard Cover — *191 Pages - $19.95*

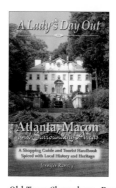

"A LADY'S DAY OUT IN ATLANTA, MACON AND SURROUNDING AREAS"

The breathtaking beauty of the North Georgia Mountains, the sophistication of Atlanta and the rich history of the Historic Heartland region are all featured in this must-have shopping guide and tourist handbook. Visitors and locals alike will enjoy the delightful stories that guide you to the best shopping, lodging, dining and luxury services, as well as exciting attractions and entertainment. This book is the perfect companion when visiting Atlanta and Macon, as well as Athens, Blue Ridge, Bolingbroke, Buckhead, Canton, Cave Spring, Cleveland, Covington, Dahlonega, Dawsonville, Decatur, Helen, Juliette, Madison, Marietta, Milledgeville, Newnan, Old Town Sharpsburg, Perry, Pine Mountain, Rome, Roswell, Sautee Nacoochee, Smyrna, Social Circle, Stone Mountain, Warm Springs, Warner Robins, Watkinsville and Woodstock. Hard Cover — *325 Pages - $19.95*

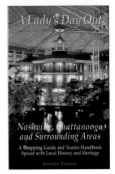

"A LADY'S DAY OUT IN NASHVILLE, CHATTANOOGA AND SURROUNDING AREAS"

From the rolling hills and mountains to Music City USA or the world's largest freshwater aquarium, Tennessee has got it going on! Discover Tennessee like you've never experienced it, with the help of our 19th book. "A Lady's Day Out in Nashville, Chattanooga and Surrounding Areas." You'll find the best shopping, lodging, eating and pampering services that each town has to offer, while learning the area's history, its special attractions, its extraordinary people and its calendar of events. This book is a must-have for those planning a getaway to: Nashville, Chattanooga, Bell Buckle, Brentwood, Clarksville, Clifton, Cookeville, Crossville, Dickson, Fayetteville, Franklin, Gallatin, Goodlettsville, Hendersonville, Lawrenceburg, Lebanon, Leipers Fork, Lynchburg, Murfreesboro, Pickwick, Savannah, Shelbyville, Signal Mountain and Waynesboro. Hard Cover — *280 Pages - $19.95*

"A LADY'S DAY OUT IN DALLAS AND SURROUNDING AREAS"

From the glitz and glamour of Dallas to the Historic Square of Gainesville, we found the most delightful shopping, scrumptious dinning, luxurious bed & breakfasts and inns and so much more! Let us guide you through the Big "D" and 20 charming surrounding towns and cities. This book is a must for visitors and "Dallas Natives" alike. Featuring Dallas and the enchanting towns of Allen, Carrollton, Cedar Hill, Coppell, DeSoto, Duncanville, Flower Mound, Forney, Frisco, Gainesville, Garland, Irving, Lancaster, Lewisville, McKinney, Plano, Richardson, Rockwall, Sherman & Waxahachie. Hard Cover — *270 Pages - $19.95*

"A LADY'S DAY OUT ON NORTHWEST FLORIDA'S EMERALD COAST"

Sparkling, emerald green waters along miles of pristine sugar white sand beaches make the Emerald Coast breathtaking! You'll find beach-side restaurants, shopping treasures, relaxing accommodations and sun-kissed attractions among the unhurried world along the Gulf. This book is the perfect companion guide to adventurers exploring the warmth and hospitality of Apalachicola, Carillon Beach, Destin, Fort Walton Beach, Grayton Beach, Gulf Breeze, Mexico Beach, Navarre Beach, Niceville, Pace, Panama City Beach, Pensacola, Pensacola Beach, Port St. Joe, Rosemary Beach, Sandestin, Santa Rosa Beach, Seagrove Beach, Seaside, Shalimar and Valparaiso. — *237 Pages - $19.95*

"A LADY'S DAY OUT IN TEXAS, VOL. III"

Features 37 new "GET-A-WAY" Texas towns—most are new and not covered in Texas, Vol. II—brimming with fascinating history and delightful, unique shopping. Inside you'll find all the details about romantic bed & breakfasts and inns, fabulous antique shops, lovely art galleries, home décor, gift shops and exciting entertainment, tearooms, soda fountains and much more. — *276 Pages - $18.95*

Book Order Form
A Lady's Day Out

PO Box 79608 • Fort Worth, Texas 76179-0608
817-236-5250 or 1-888-860-ALDO (2536)

Please send _____ copies of **"A LADY'S DAY OUT IN TEXAS, VOL. IV"** at $19.95 per copy, plus $4.00 S/H for each book ordered. (Tax included.)

Please send _____ copies of **"A LADY'S DAY OUT IN THE TEXAS HILL COUNTRY, VOL. III"** at $19.95 per copy, plus $4.00 S/H for each book ordered. (Tax included.)

Please send _____ copies of **"A LADY'S DAY OUT IN SAN ANTONIO & SURROUNDING AREAS, VOL. II"** at $19.95 per copy, plus $4.00 S/H for each book ordered. (Tax included.)

Please send _____ copies of **"A LADY'S DAY OUT IN ATLANTA, MACON & SURROUNDING AREAS"** at $19.95 per copy, plus $4.00 S/H for each book ordered. (Tax included.)

Please send _____ copies of **"A LADY'S DAY OUT IN DALLAS & SURROUNDING AREAS, VOL. II"** at $19.95 per copy, plus $4.00 S/H for each book ordered. (Tax included.)

Please send _____ copies of **"A LADY'S DAY OUT IN NASHVILLE, CHATTANOOGA & SURROUNDING AREAS"** at $19.95 per copy, plus $4.00 S/H for each book ordered. (Tax included.)

Please send _____ copies of **"A LADY'S DAY OUT ON NORTHWEST FLORIDA'S EMERALD COAST"** at $19.95 per copy, plus $4.00 S/H for each book ordered. (Tax included.)

Please send _____ copies of **"A LADY'S DAY OUT IN THE RIO GRANDE VALLEY & SOUTH PADRE ISLAND"** at $17.95 per copy, plus $4.00 S/H for each book ordered. (Tax included.)

Please send _____ copies of **"A LADY'S DAY OUT IN TEXAS, VOL. III"** at $18.95 per copy, plus $4.00 S/H for each book ordered. (Tax included.)

MAIL BOOKS TO:

NAME: _____

ADDRESS: _____

CITY_____ STATE_____ ZIP_____

AMOUNT ENCLOSED: _____

www.ALadysDayOut.com • info@ALadysDayOut.com

A Lady's Day Out

IN

TEXAS

VOLUME IV

A Shopping Guide & Tourist Handbook

— featuring —

Bryan / College Station • Calvert • Carthage
Goldthwaite • Granbury • Grapevine • Henderson
Kilgore • Lampasas • Mineola • Salado
San Saba • Weatherford

by Jennifer Ramsey

Cover features Abigaile's Treehouse
(See related story on page 191.)

CREDITS

Editor/Author
Jennifer Ramsey

Director of Research & Sales
Jennifer Ramsey

Administrative & Production
Kay Payne

Editor & Writer
Gena Maselli

Contributing Writers
Jenny Harper Nahoum
Gena Maselli
Laura Pender

Copyright 2011
A Lady's Day Out, Inc.
ISBN 13: 978-1-891527-20-3
ISBN 10: 1-891527-20-7

Paid advertising by invitation only.

Produced by

A Lady's Day Out

Layout by Jill Dowling
Armstrong Printing Company, Austin, Texas

Table of Contents

Note from the Author

Twenty years! As of the writing of this introduction, *A Lady's Day Out* is celebrating 20 years in business. Amazing! I have been honored and blessed to share my adventures and tell my tales with readers throughout all these years. As with each publication, months and months are spent on the road, away from my children, my garden and my life. All of this would have been nearly impossible but for two things: the townspeople we visit and our following of appreciative readers. The people in my travels open their gracious arms of hospitality and welcome me wholeheartedly into their charming towns. They always make me feel at home. And, the glowing feedback we receive from the wives, mothers, girlfriends, grandmothers and even some gentleman, reaffirm that what we do is important and appreciated. Readers are quick to share how these books are invaluable to their explorations and how they too are inspired by the entrepreneurial spirit that radiates from each story.

In this latest edition, *A Lady's Day Out in Texas Vol. IV,* I found myself revisiting several Texas towns featured in previous publications. Some towns outshined the others and only the best ones made the book! How fascinating it is to watch these towns stretch and bend with the times. Building upon what made them a destination decades ago. In Salado, for example, wine making and tasting has hit the stage. I was in for the latter but have always wanted to try the former, as well! And, speaking of the stage, there are now venues for live entertainment in Salado, usually on the weekends, like The Silver Spur Theater. Bryan/College Station, Granbury, Grapevine, Mineola and several others are also bringing in top entertainment.

Other towns, which have never before been included in any of our books, have become appealing enough to showcase as new destinations. Kilgore, Carthage, Henderson and San Saba, are tremendous examples with little bustling downtown areas, marvelous museums and fascinating people. Calvert is another small "first timer" town with 47 blocks on the National Register of Historic Places and an up-and-coming art community in the downtown shopping area.

For those who have not met me personally, I am a talker. But, along with the gift of gab, I am an excellent listener. You see, I come from a long line of skilled storytellers. As a child, I remember frequently hiding under kitchen tables for hours, just so I could listen while my grandparents, aunts and uncles, and parents wove their tales. Great practice for both listening and storytelling, I suppose. With such a heritage, it's no wonder 20 years seems to have flown by while working on the *A Lady's Day Out* book series. Now, I am sharing these fascinating towns and delightful people with each one of our readers, through the stories in this book. You will surely be as enchanted with these towns as I was. Have fun, enjoy your trips and let us know how they turn out.

With so many books still to write, here's to another fascinating 20 years—we are going to need it!

Be sure and visit www.ALadysDayOut.com for updates and book-signing schedules!

Jenni

Texas....
Wide-open Spaces with a Twist

Texas! Rodeos, oil wells, wildflowers, Big Tex, pro football, high fashion, music, beautiful beaches, wineries, cowboys, oil rigs, longhorn cattle, The Alamo, barbecue, The Twelfth Man, Bevo, mockingbirds, tumbleweeds and sweet tea. How can a Texan even begin to describe this larger-than-life state where Southern hospitality is still rolled out to visitors with great pride? Texans *are* proud. They like being known for the wide-open spaces, spectacular natural resources and diverse beauty of their land, and for the fierce determination, character, perseverance and genuine friendliness of its people. In fact, Texas was originally named "Tejas" which means "friends" or "allies."

When people visualize Texas, it is often wide-open spaces with cactus and longhorn cattle. You'll certainly find that during your visit here, but the state is as diverse as the many cultures it has embraced, as colorful as the azaleas that bloom in the east and as spirited as its football. It is a grand place that is a wonder to discover.

We have been out and about discovering Texas for many years; delighted at the beauty of the different regions and unique personalities of the towns. From the white, sandy beaches of the Gulf Coast and piney woods in the east, to sophisticated big cities famous for fashion and glamour and wide-open lands in the west, we've visited, shopped and eaten our way almost across the entire state. This is our fourth volume of A Lady's Day Out in Texas because we continue to find incredible areas we know you will love.

We have covered many of the large cities in previous books,

but chose this time to visit some of the wonderful tucked-away small towns and cities that are exciting to shop and visit. Read the introduction information before each chapter to learn the history and get an idea of the true "flavor" and unique opportunities in each town. You're going to love discovering these delightful little pocket communities in Texas.

In **Central Texas,** we explored the college towns of **Bryan and College Station**, as well as Calvert and Salado. One word of advice here: "If you're bleeding, it better be *maroon!*" Texas A&M University and "Aggie Spirit" reign unchallenged in Bryan and College Station, so before you leave you're certain to learn the word "whoop." Conservative, conventional, old-fashioned, but with a zest for fun and entertainment, these communities hold fast to family and tradition. Fall means football here, and fans pour in from everywhere to stand (they literally stand the entire game) as the "12th Man" for their beloved Aggies. Downtown Bryan is undergoing a remarkable revitalization, and there is a huge movement in the area towards the arts. In fact, there are incredible art galleries and museums located on the A&M Campus that are open to the public, including the George H. W. Bush (41st) Presidential Library. You will recognize a little of the "Austin influence" here, not only in art, but in music as well.

As a side trip from here be sure to find the quaint town of **Calvert**. It's located just a few miles from Bryan/College Station and is beginning to make a name for itself in the arts. With 37 blocks of the town in the National Historic Register, there is obviously a commitment to the town's historical preservation.

Slow down between Austin and Waco, so you don't miss the opportunity to spend a little time in the charming **Village of Salado**. What used to be just a quaint little stop along the highway is emerging as both a destination shopping community and popular get-a-way. It's full of history, wonderful little tearooms and shops and really nice people. Many of the businesses here were threatened in 2010 when Tropical Storm Hermine dropped 16 inches of rain on Salado Creek, literally washing some downstream. With true Texas grit, they have all pulled together to reopen with smiles on their faces and bright hopes for the future. With new restaurants, bed and breakfasts and even wineries opening, it is an enchanting place to explore and enjoy.

In **North Texas,** we found the absolutely charming towns of Granbury, Weatherford and Grapevine. With such close proximity to Dallas and Ft. Worth, this entire area is thriving; growing in both population and sophistication. These communities take pride in being able to retain their individual small-town charm and personalities while benefitting from all of the excitement of their larger and more well-known Metroplex neighbors. Each is a perfect day trip from Dallas or Ft. Worth, offering great shopping and dining opportunities, remarkable historic sites and beautiful gardens to explore. North Texas is also emerging as a wine destination, attracting visitors from across the country. It is an area filled with lots of interesting Texas history, frontier legends and folklore; yet is contemporary, well dressed and sophisticated. So much fun to discover!

The good life in **Granbury** includes beautiful Lake Granbury and all of the fun that goes along with it. Wonderful fun in the sun, days on the beach, river cruises, boating, skiing and fishing are attracting a large number of retirees and new business owners. This Brazos Jewel glitters with fabulous shopping, delightful hide away bed and breakfasts, and a toe-tapping "Branson-like" atmosphere. Considered one of the 100 "Great Towns in America," Granbury is rich in history, the arts, entertainment and recreation, but has old-fashioned, small-town values that you will love.

A little more rustic and a bit more Western, **Weatherford** welcomes visitors with lots of pride and tradition. The downtown square is a great place to discover the heartbeat of the town. Put a few quarters in the parking meters and explore this charming haven from one end to the other. This Texas "peach capital" and "cutting horse capital" is also home to two spectacular gardens, a fascinating cultural center and an abundance of Queen Ann and Victorian historic homes. It was home to famous movie stars and internationally known artists, as well as the colorful, legendary cattle drivers Oliver Loving and Charles Goodnight (inspiration for McMurtry's Lonesome Dove rangers).

Devine **Grapevine** has become a trendy, premier leisure destination in North Texas with a little something for everyone, including exciting vintage train rides, fabulous Opry musical entertainment and a downtown filled with fantastic shops, boutiques and restaurants. It's "a little Country Western with a Tuscan twist." Locals say that their charming town is "aged to perfection" and with a name like Grapevine, they know they are right. It is the center of the North Texas wine trail, with fabulous wineries that include rustic farmhouses and French-style chateaus. You can stomp your way through the countryside wineries during the harvest and celebrate the yield of the fields at exciting wine festivals.

If you're looking for Mayberry, USA head to **East Texas**! In particular, the interesting small towns of Kilgore, Mineola, Henderson and Carthage. You'll feel as though you have truly traveled back in time in this slow-paced piney woods part of Texas that is so unlike its northern and western neighbors. These communities are cornucopias of unique shopping and eating opportunities, filled with exciting treasures and some of the friendliest Texans you will meet. You'll "strike it rich" in these East Texas towns as you discover all of the wonderful things we've chronicled through these chapters. Have fun!

Mineola takes great pride in its wonderful history and has found a beautiful way to preserve that old-fashioned, small-town feel of yesteryear. The downtown is illuminated with soft, beautiful period lighting, and the result is charming. Locals set their clocks by train whistles, enjoy wonderful live theatre and feast on the legendary East Texas Burgers.

A larger-than-life statue of Tex Ritter and his horse, White Flash, welcome folks to **Carthage**, home to the Texas Country Music Hall of Fame. This town celebrates in a big way, honoring some of the biggest country music entertainers in the country. You just might agree with locals who say they are the "Best Small Town in Texas!"

The National Register Downtown Historical Square of **Henderson** is one of the most picturesque downtown squares in East Texas. Upscale shopping, two great museums, wildflower trails, syrup festivals and a beautiful lake make this tucked-away town a great place to stay and play.

From the famous high-kicking "Rangerettes" to the 80 plus lighted oil derricks that put the town on the map—**Kilgore** has quite a history. Kilgore is home to "the world's richest acre" named for one of the most famous oil discoveries in the United States. It is also famous for the beautiful Kilgore College Rangerettes, talented ambassadors who have represented the spirit of Texas football throughout the country and the world with their famous dance routines and high kicks. Add wonderful Shakespearean theatre and a lively downtown shopping experience and you have one fun small town!

Head at last to one of our favorite places in all of Texas—the remarkable **Hill Country**. This area of the Lone Star State is incredibly beautiful and intoxicating. Picturesque farms and ranches dot the rolling hillside—gorgeous wildflowers wow travelers and small-town pleasures delight and tempt visitors to never leave. It's a fisherman's and hunter's paradise, a place of history and heritage and a shopper's dream. There are so many fascinating places to explore in the beautiful Hill Country, but in this volume, we have chosen to spotlight the three small towns of San Saba, Lampasas and Goldthwaite.

Historical **San Saba** is known as the Pecan Capital of the World, populated with pecan trees that could possibly date back to Columbus' discovery of America. In fact, the welcome sign to San Saba is a red, white and blue Texas flag in the shape of a pecan tree! The beautiful land here is both rolling hills and rugged woods, blessed and fed by the San Saba and Colorado Rivers. It's a quaint and charming place to shop and visit.

Goldthwaite (a tongue twister) stands at the entrance to the beautiful Hill Country, and considers itself to be a progressive community with rural roots that run deep. It's the county seat of Mills County and home to the Regency Suspension Bridge, one of only two remaining historical suspension bridges open to public traffic. It, too, is a fun little Texas town to discover.

Lampasas (last but not least) is a historical town known for the many beautiful mineral springs throughout the area whose waters are said to possess healing properties. These springs attracted many Indian tribes long before the white settlers arrived, and continue today to draw visitors with cold swimming holes, great fishing, whitewater rafting and bird watching.

Even though there are many wonderful outdoor recreational opportunities in these small Hill Country towns, they also have downtowns and pockets that sparkle with specialty shops, galleries and eateries that will surprise and delight.

So put on your comfy shoes, grab your camera and several large shopping bags and get ready to discover these four wonderful little pockets of Texas. You'll fall in love with the diverse beauty of each area, and feel drawn to the lovely people who are lucky enough to live there. You will understand the fierce loyalty and passion of Texans who proudly proclaim that that everything is "bigger and better" in their small slices of heaven, who whoop and holler with fiery spirit for their football players and who still like to "porch set" until the sun goes down. Explore the downtown squares, sip great wine, bait a hook, discover "black gold," eat a whole peach pie and fill up your shopping bags with unique treasures.

Get ready to fall in love with small-town Texas. We have!

North Texas

Granbury

Grapevine

Weatherford

Discover Granbury

The folks who get to call Granbury "home" just can't stop smiling. They think they are the luckiest people in Texas. We agree! The relaxed lifestyle and community spirit, the blue waters of beautiful Lake Granbury, rich frontier and Texas history, wonderful theatre and live entertainment venues, excellent shopping and dining opportunities and locals who are friendly and welcoming are all part of the charisma of this small, thriving Texas jewel.

It's called the "**Jewel of the Brazos**," branded as a place "Where Texas History Lives," and was voted one of "America's Most Charming Towns and Villages." Granbury is a beautiful place to spend a weekend, though you'll want to stay for a lifetime. It is said that Granbury has exchanged its slow horse and buggy strolls from the 1800s for a full-throttle gallop—a town that holds to its frontier legacy of exciting Wild West outlaws and historical charm but is thrilled with its fast-growing popularity and national recognition. It is a perfect vacation destination, with something for everyone. Not many small towns can boast a lake winding through their downtown district, a bevy of wineries and bed and breakfasts, a historic opera house and musical theatre of which even Nashville would approve, a state university and at least one party or festival every month. You can start the day on the blue waters of the Brazos, explore the downtown businesses and boutiques, then treat yourself to a great dinner and an evening of live theater. It's the "Granbury Good Life!"

The Legend of Granbury

You will discover that Granbury is a city rich in Texas history and frontier folklore. Even though the charming downtown square is filled today with locals and visitors enjoying the quaint boutiques, antique stores and art galleries, it is easy to imagine it during the early days when legends like Jesse James, Belle Star or even John Wilkes Booth walked the dusty streets.

Hood County came into existence in 1866, and the small community sprang up within its borders, but Granbury's history actually dates back to 1854 when "Uncle Tommy" Lambert and Amon Bond led a group of pioneers across the Brazos River to its west bank. J. and J.H. Nutt donated 40 acres of riverfront property for a new county seat and Hood County was formed. The town of Granbury was then named for Brig. Gen. Hiram Bronson Granbury, who led Confederate troops from this area during the Civil War. He was one of the six Confederate generals killed at the Battle of Franklin on November 20, 1864.

In the beginning, the town consisted of a square and a log cabin courthouse, and many of the original buildings are now registered historic landmarks. As in many small frontier towns, the arrival of the railroad brought many changes. The Fort Worth and Rio Grande Railway came through Granbury in 1887, and prompted the construction of many limestone buildings in the downtown area. Today, there are 39 historic buildings on the courthouse square, and many of those house the businesses you will read about in our book. For instance, the old Opera House, which was built in 1886, is a main tourist attraction, and the old red brick train depot is now a museum. Some were saloons (many in fact,) gun shops, the sheriff's office, general stores and feed stores. Granbury's beautiful downtown square was the first town square in Texas to be listed on the National Register of Historic Places, and has become a prototype for small town restorations across America.

Fact & Folklore & Legends

Granbury is a town with lots of great folklore, and one of the best places to learn its colorful history is at the **Hood County Museum**, which is open on weekends. See the original jail cells and learn the stories of the town's famous citizens. One of those famous Granbury legends is that of the infamous outlaw Jesse James.

Is he really buried in the Granbury Cemetery? Well the headstone reads; Jesse Woodson James, September 5, 1847- August 15, 1951. Born the son of a Baptist minister, the outlaw Jesse James, was known to ride with Quantrill's Raiders during the Civil War, raiding Northern towns for profit. He also robbed banks and trains and was supposedly shot and killed in Missouri. In Texas, however, the long-standing legend says that he, in fact, faked his death, moved to Texas and died in Granbury at the age of 104. The folks of Granbury hold fast to this story!

Crockett Street in Granbury is named in honor of the Davy Crockett family and their contributions to Hood County History. Davy's widow Elizabeth and their son Robert settled here during the 1850s, and her grandson, Ashley Crockett, was Granbury's first newspaper publisher during the early 1870s.

Also big on the "Granbury Legends" list is the story of John Wilkes Booth, who supposedly lived in Granbury during the 1870s under the name of John St. Helen. The man known as St. Helen worked as a saloon bartender in several of the downtown buildings, and was always believed to be the man who shot and killed President Abraham Lincoln. Even though Booth was supposedly killed in Virginia, legend has it that he escaped and found his way to the South, and eventually to Granbury. It is even believed that Booth (St. Helen) once performed Shakespeare in the Opera House. Again, Granbury locals like this version!

During your venture into history in Granbury, don't miss the **U.S. Veterans Museum**, with exhibits of military artifacts from almost every war in American history. Weapons, uniforms, photos, flags, maps and artwork from the War of 1812, the Civil War, World Wars I and II, the Korean War, Vietnam and Desert Storm memorialize the U.S. veterans who served and sacrificed for their country.

Now Showing! In Granbury

Folks in Granbury surely have no trouble finding exciting entertainment and adventure. From professional productions and toe-tapping musicals at the Granbury Opera House and Granbury Live theatre to family nights in an old-fashioned drive-in, this is one of the liveliest theater communities in small-town America. **Granbury Opera House**, which is a designated Texas State Historic Site, was built in 1886 when formal theatre was first introduced to the frontier. Even on the wild Texas frontier, culture was not forgotten, and often the most splendid building in town was an "opera house." Granbury was proud of its fancy theater that attracted traveling vaudeville acts, minstrel shows and magicians. Renovated and reopened in 1975, the beautiful stone building features exposed stone walls, original doors, period chandeliers and authentic needlepoint seats reminiscent of its early days. It serves today as a springboard for talented young professionals and aspiring performers, with Broadway productions and community theatre.

And, who doesn't remember the days when the entire family piled into the car for a move at "the drive-in?" Well, Granbury still has one! The old-fashioned **Brazos Drive-In Theater** is a step back in time, a place where you can pack the lawn chairs and bring the children and grandparents for a night at the movies on the large screen. A 1950s original style concession stand serves homemade "movie food," and there is always a double feature on the weekend.

The Good Life in Granbury

In 1969, the creation of **Lake Granbury** on the Brazos River ignited a land rush for weekend homes, new businesses and a terrific population boom. The 8,700-acre lake has 103 miles of shoreline—perfect for boating, skiing and year-round fishing. With such great lake access for water sports, Granbury has become a favorite destination for family vacations. It is also becoming a popular retirement community because of its relaxed lifestyle and small-town hospitality.

If your idea of fun is action; rent a jet ski, boat or kayak, tee off on a nearby championship golf course, or hike or bike through trails in the rolling hills. Dining opportunities abound in Granbury, from rustic "**Line Camp**" steakhouses to "**Babe's**" chicken dinner houses and everything in between. And, for wine aficionados, there are beautiful wineries and tasting rooms that specialize in delicious Texas wines and great musical entertainment. The green and yellow Granbury Trolley connects hotels, restaurants and attractions so hop on board and explore it all.

Granbury loves a party! And, they do it often! Community celebrations include **Gen. Hiram Granbury's birthday celebration** in March, The **Harvest Moon Festival** in October, **The Christmas**

Parade in November, **The Candlelight Tour of Homes**, and everyone's favorite the Granbury Chamber of Commerce **Fourth of July Festival**, that draws more than 60,000 visitors for parades, food and, of course, fireworks.

"Grand" Granbury Shopping

Antiques stores, Western wear, book nooks, quilting shops, art galleries, jewelry and so much more! Granbury is a shopper's delight. Wander around the square, and in and out of restaurants and boutiques. Get an ice cream cone or cup of freshly brewed coffee and a slice of pie. Try a decadent piece of fudge or find a unique treasure in the "girly pink" **Pamela and Co.** Gentlemen-in-waiting can use the bench in front of **Stuff~N~Nonsense** while you browse, then head to the **Pearl Street Station** for a bowl of spicy gumbo. You will love meeting the shopkeepers who grew up in Granbury and agree with the others who decided later it was the perfect place for their business. Find the wonderful shops just outside the square and rest and renew in the many fabulous bed and breakfasts and country inns. Read our "stories behind the stores" in Granbury, and then have fun discovering all of their wonderful treasures. We did! *(Color photo featured in front section of book.)*

For additional information on Granbury, contact the Granbury Convention & Visitors Bureau at 682-936-1200, 877-936-1201 or visit www.granburytx.com.

March
> General Granbury's Birthday

April
> Granbury Wine Walk

May
> An Affair of the Arts – Downtown Artwalk
> Memorial Day Hometown & Picnic Festival

July
> 4th of July Festival

September
> Last Saturday Gallery Night
> Gunsmoke on the Brazos

October
> Last Saturday Gallery Night
> Vettes on the Square
> Taste of Granbury
> Harvest Moon Festival
> Granbury Quilt Guild

November
> Christmas Country Parade n Lights

December
> Candlelight Tour of Homes

Antiques

Bob and Cherry Hanneman are both retired "railroaders" that followed their passion for antiques and opened their own store. Cherry says, "Twenty-something years ago, we purchased our first antiques—a pair of black marble-top night stands which still sit in our guest room. With that first purchase, we were hooked!" Brazos Moon in Granbury is located at 124 N. Houston St. in a historic Victorian building, built by Jefferson Davis Brown in 1890. His name is still visible, chiseled into the limestone on the building. Inside there are vignettes of treasures that will impress the most avid collector, and even a section of the store nicknamed "The Man Corner," filled with new and vintage firearms, knives and tools. "One of the most interesting items we've had was a Colt Lightning .22 Rifle, used by Annie Oakley in Buffalo Bill's Wild West Show," says Bob. The Hannemans are proud of their dedicated vendors that offer quality selections of furniture, glassware, textiles, jewelry and more. Visit www.brazosmoon.com or call 817-579-8202.

Artèfactz

The path to becoming a serious artist is never easy. It takes years of artistic mastery, a dose of business savvy and unwavering determination. That's the path that led Cynthia James to open Artèfactz at 120 N. Houston St. in Granbury.

After graduating with a BA in Art Education, Cynthia worked as a contemporary artist, jewelry designer and sculptor. She went on to live and work abroad, specializing in glass, metal and clay. Her work is shown throughout the United States and as far away as Japan. Though she dreamed of owning her own gallery, it wasn't until she was flying back to the States that she decided to become a serious, working artist. Over the next several years, she built her jewelry and sculpture clientele, and eventually bought the gallery where she worked.

Cynthia's gallery, Artèfactz, showcases art from several local artisans. Her own work includes stunning dichroic fused glass jewelry, which serves as inspiration for her larger pieces. "Dichroic means two colors, depending upon the angle from which it is viewed," she explains, "The technique enables me to create jewelry with the effect similar to the iridescence of a butterfly's wings or fire opals."

In addition to Cynthia's work, Artèfactz offers purses by Miche Bag; handmade bears by BB French; children's clothing by designers like Laura Smith of Lullaby Couture, Nita Vaughn of Freckles & Frills Creations, as well as the very popular brand—Mudpie. Donna Alberts of Palace Toys carries a full line of toys for every age including Melissa and Doug toy company. In addition, you'll find Pam Ward's wonderful interior décor items along with her gorgeous floral arrangements. Budding artists will love the supplies and creations, as well as classes taught by fiber artist Julie Pitts of Yarn Extraordinaire. Visit www.artefactz.com or call 817-573-9446.

The Jeweler's Workshop

A working bench jeweler since 1976, Jim Patterson's name is synonymous with superb craftsmanship. He opened his first jewelry store in 1985, but his love and fascination with jewelry design and repair dates back to his early days as an employee at a chain jewelry store, "Rather than selling, I spent most of my time watching and learning from the master jeweler," he says. "One day, after the repair expert had moved away, a rush repair job came in, so I did the work. I've been happy every day since then knowing that I can make a living doing something I love so much." Jim does a large volume of repair work, but he also carries a number of custom pieces, including his wife Debbie's beautifully beaded pieces. In fact, his customers sometimes snatch up their designs before they even make it to the showcase.. The Jeweler's Workshop, 115 W. Bridge St. in Granbury, is the perfect place to find (or design!) a new creation or repair a treasured heirloom. Visit www.jpattersonjeweler.com or call 817-573-4322.

Attractions, Entertainment & Golf

Texas Family Musicals Inc.
Granbury Opera House

During the 19th century, an opera house was a true mark of civilization in a small frontier town. When the theater movement swept through the country, Granbury was proud to open its doors in 1886 to Kerr's Hall, built on the south side of Granbury's historic square at 116 S. Pearl St. Restored in 1975, and listed on the National Register of Historic Places the fabulous Granbury Opera House today features professional live theater including smash musicals, plays and melodramas starring some of the country's most talented performers. With its balcony, period chandeliers and wall sconces, the Opera House retains the charm and atmosphere of its original décor, and is called "The Crown Jewel of Granbury." The Texas Family Musical Series produces such hit shows as The Johnny Cash Show; "It's a Wonderful Life," "The Night the Music Died," "Greater Tuna," and Broadway Magic to sold-out crowds. Call 817-573-9191 or visit www.granburyoperahouse.net.

HIDDEN OAKS
The Golf Course in Granbury

Your significant "golfer" won't mind a trip to Granbury while you poke through antique stores and boutiques, or linger over lunch with the girls. He can head straight to the greens and enjoy 18 holes of golf at Hidden Oaks. This public championship course features tree-lined fairways, meandering streams and placid lakes, as well as a four-tier driving range and putting green. Hidden Oaks is well known for its award-winning junior golf program. Blood, sweat and a few happy tears went into the construction of this spectacular course. In fact, Owner and PGA Golf Pro Rex Worrell spent two years building it himself. Another PGA Golf Pro, Jarrott Hampton, manages Hidden Oaks, too. Jarrott is proud of Hidden Oaks' reputation and the quality, and affordable, golf experience it offers to local and out-of-town golfers. Hidden Oaks is located at 2701 Hideaway Bay Ct. Call 817-279-1078 or visit www.hiddenoaksgolf.net.

Granbury Resort Conference Center

A literal "wall of windows" allow guests at the Granbury Resort Conference Center beautiful views of Lake Granbury, The Boardwalk and a white sandy beach that is perfect for outdoor activities and events. Located at 621 E. Pearl St, this state-of-the-art, two-story rock building has 20,000 square feet of meeting space and can accommodate up to 650 guests with additional meeting space outdoors. Since its grand opening, the center has been a popular venue for corporate events and conventions up to 350 delegates, weddings and receptions. Onsite catering, audiovisual services and high-speed Internet make the Center perfect for business seminars and conferences. There is also a new Hilton Garden Inn adjacent to the Center that's connected by the boardwalk overlooking Lake Granbury, so groups can meet and stay together. Call 682-936-1201, 877-936-1201 or visit www.granburytx.com/conventioncenter.

Bed and Breakfasts, Cabins & Cottages

The Windmill Farm and Bed & Breakfast

"History in motion." That's how Chuck and Ruby Rickgauer describe their pastoral, countryside ranch. The Windmill Farm and Bed & Breakfast, 6625 Colony Rd. between Tolar and Granbury, draws visitors from across the country to catch a glimpse of the 42 magnificent, antique windmills that line the property's driveway. The first windmill was brought from Ruby's parents' farm in South Dakota, for decoration. Chuck soon began finding other windmills (some from the 1880s) to add to his collection. What started as an *"If you build it, they will come"* story has become a wonderful Americana exhibit. The three cabins that overlook the ranch, each named for a historic windmill, have covered porches and rocking chairs and are perfect for enjoying the beautiful sunrises and sunsets. Guests love the peaceful environment, but they adore Ruby's homemade hot cinnamon rolls and delicious cherry pie! Visit www.thewindmillfarm.com or call 254-835-4168 or 817-279-2217.

Granbury Gardens
Bed & Breakfast

Kay Wasielewski had wanted to own a bed and breakfast for 25 years, so when she and husband Stan found the historic home at 321 W. Doyle St., they decided it was time to make that dream come true. Granbury Gardens is located in the original "Craftsman Home" of James H. Doyle, Granbury's first merchant. It was built in 1911 from plans published in *Ladies Home Journal*. Just off Granbury's historic square, this lovely home offers guests a peaceful, romantic retreat amid stately trees, lush gardens, water features and Koi ponds. Each of the four guestrooms has its own private bath and wireless DSL. Easy access to the garden allows you to enjoy a glass of wine in the hot tub, or in front of the outdoor fireplace on a cool evening. But the best part of the stay here may be Kay's famous gourmet breakfasts. They've received rave reviews from as far away as England! Call 817-573-9010 or visit www.granburygardens.com.

GRANBURY Log Cabins

TEXAS HERITAGE GUESTHOUSE

After a day of shopping Granbury's fabulous downtown or enjoying the nearby lake, come relax in the peaceful countryside in the historic Granbury Log Cabins, 5801 Matlock Rd. You will feel as though you have stepped back in time—back to 1867 when pioneer Lemuel Stone built this dogtrot house (two log cabins linked by a breezeway) in East Texas from massive trees felled and hewn with a single axe. Owners John and Ona Pruitt spent two years moving the cabins to their land and reconstructing the structures log by log. Rocking chairs provide hours of old-fashioned front-porch "settin." Or, you can take a leisurely stroll around the property. Each cabin contains a queen bed and a sleeping loft for children, large private bath, television, microwave and refrigerator. A continental breakfast is included. Visit www.granbury-log-cabins.com or call 817-326-3639.

BABE'S COTTAGE
MIN'S COTTAGE

After enjoying all that beautiful Granbury has to offer, find your home away from home in one of two private, cozy cottages owned by Dutch and Brenda Wilkinson. Sip your morning coffee from the old-fashioned screened porch of **Babe's Cottage**, a charming two-bedroom house with commanding views of the open water of Lake Granbury and the historic Hood County Courthouse steeple. The three-bedroom **Min's Cottage** located next door also shares the premier waterfront location. Both are close to the public boat ramp—perfect for fun-filled days of fishing, boating and skiing—just minutes from Granbury's historic downtown square. Both cottages have completely furnished kitchens, linens, Wi-Fi and cable television, and are decorated with all the comforts of home. Try your luck with a fishing pole out back or plan a backyard picnic by the lake. The Cottages are rented daily, weekly, monthly or even for the year, so you can plan a wonderful visit to Granbury. Visit www.plantationinngranbury.com or call Plantation Inn, 817-573-8846. *(See related story page 37.)*

Books

It's exactly the type of bookstore you might imagine on the historic square in a small town. Children cozy up in the corner to read, tourists find a treasure for their cookbook collection and locals stop in for books they've ordered. Books on the Square, 121 E. Bridge St., is located on the ground floor of The Historic Nutt House Hotel filled with shelves of wonderful books, including a great Texana collection, popular cookbooks, best sellers and rare finds. As a retired librarian, from Granbury ISD, Melinda Ray's love of books and history is evident throughout the bookstore, where she also carries a great selection of greeting cards and special gifts. Books on the Square has also become a destination for a decadent midday treat where you can tantalize your senses and warm your soul with a great book and a yummy bag of peanut brittle or pecan toffee—also the perfect addition to any gift. For more information, call 817-573-9672. *(See related story on page 37.)*

The Wedding Connection promises to make your wedding as stress-free as possible! This full-service wedding planning business, 515 S. Morgan St., was opened in 2001 and over the years, has assembled an award-winning team. This talented group of 19 professionals will join forces to make your wedding day the best day of your life! And, the best part? You only pay for the services you select! They believe that your wedding day should be everything you've always dreamed it would be. That's why they promise to listen to your desires—and budget—so that your wedding is as unique as you are.

Whether you want the entire wedding planned, or just a little help on the wedding weekend, **Something Blue Weddings** will be there! This fabulous team has garnered praise from happy couples who say their wedding was a once in a lifetime, memorable event!

The team at **Fleur de Lis Designs** has an obvious passion and love for what they do—creative floral designs. Whether you desire your wedding to be elegant and romantic or vibrant and fun, Fleur de Lis Designs will make it happen.

And, who could forget about the cake? Award-winning **Granbury Cakes** custom designs each creation to fit every wish. Its signature White Chocolate Chip Cake, is positively divine! The staff promises to combine your great ideas and flavor choice with its creative expertise to make an utterly stunning (and scrumptious!) centerpiece.

The Wedding Connection plans weddings nationwide, as well as destination weddings. Their specialty, however, is the "West-o-Plex" (DFW) weddings! Visit www.theweddingconnectiongroup.com or call 817-573-3332.

Fashion & Accessories

A Granbury tradition since 1978, this stellar ladies' boutique continues to be a favorite for stylish gals of all ages. Jeans Crossing, 1442 E. Hwy. 377, is a beautiful store that is a joy to shop, a compliment that owner Carolyn Moore hears all the time. Carolyn has been a part of the store since 1979, first as an employee and then as an owner. In fact, her late husband used to say, "Why don't you just buy the store?" Her standard response was always, "I can't," but when the former owner made her an offer she couldn't refuse, she jumped at it. Carolyn is proud to carry on the wonderful reputation and tradition of Granbury's oldest ladies' boutique. She says, "We have great fashions and accessories for girls ages 20 to 80." Jeans Crossing is a designated Brighton Heart store and carries selections from Tribal, G Designs, Ivy Jane, Uncle Frank, Krista Lee, Kut Denim, French Dressing and Honey Bee Footwear. For more information, call 817-573-3112.

Becky Barton has been dressing the stylish ladies of Granbury since 1990 when she opened Stuff~N~Nonsense Boutique at 113 W. Bridge St. The eclectic, fashion-forward boutique is just off the historic square in a charming ivy-covered cottage. There is even a bench for the gentlemen-in-waiting. Becky has a keen eye for quality and a definite flair for style. She loves finding gorgeous fashions that everyone can afford. She carries unusual jewelry and fashion accessories and wonderful missy fashions, including "FDJ" French Dressing Jeans, which donates a portion of every sale to breast cancer research. Becky and her staff are committed to fundraising, and even host an annual Pink Ribbon Luncheon/Style Show for the Susan G. Komen Foundation. You'll also be charmed by "Foxy," her adorable, furry partner she adopted while hosting a "doggie/person" style show benefiting Friends for Animals. Call 817-573-9060 or visit www.snn.weebly.com.

Teenagers, moms and grandmothers all love shopping this fantastic ladies' clothing boutique on the square in downtown Granbury. The Clothes Horse, 204 N. Houston St., is a wildly popular store with ladies of all ages who truly love fashion. Owner Cindy Hyde says, "Girls of all ages just want to have fun. I love helping them look beautiful while they do!" She was always a huge "clothes horse," and loved buying Western apparel, but opening The Clothes Horse in 2003 gave her the opportunity to offer the fashionable ladies of Granbury exciting, hip clothing, beautiful jewelry, fanciful footwear and fun accessories at affordable prices. She carries beautiful Pandora jewelry and popular Brighton accessories. Lines like Not Your Daughter's Jeans, Live A Little washable suede jackets, Spanx and Jessica Simpson handbags—make this a one stop shop. Fashionable styles for all ages. Call 817-573-0279. *(See related story page 33.)*

Pamela Burchfield loves her life. "I have a great, supportive husband, a wonderful son, three adorable Yorkies, I live in a beautiful home on Lake Granbury, and … I have a business that I absolutely love!" Pamela owns Bella Rosa Consignment Gallery, 1440 E. Hwy. 377. In addition to offering upscale fashion, jewelry and accessories, Bella Rosa provides great home décor, furniture and one-of-a-kind gifts. Pamela is a talented businesswoman with impeccable style and a keen eye for quality, which is evident throughout her shop. She carries only the best in ladies and teen clothing like Anthropologie and Atelier Versace, and handbags from Louis Vuitton, Prada, Coach and Brighton. To complement the clothing, you'll love her selection of new and consignment jewelry. There are fabulous finds at a fraction of retail prices.

Pamela has always loved the consignment business. She began working part time for a similar store in 1999, and then, with the help of her husband Mical, decided to open her own shop. They started small, doing all the work themselves. They have been so successful

during the last five years that they have expanded three times. Customers say it is the fine selection of upscale clothing, the attention to detail and the incredible customer service that makes Bella Rosa one of their favorite places to shop for resale or retail. Pamela never takes a day for granted, and considers every day exciting. What could be more fun than remarkable clothes and beautiful jewelry? She attributes her success to a combination of hard work, steadfast integrity, terrific employees and, of course, faithful consigners. New inventory arrives daily, so drop in often, or you may miss a special treasure. For more information, call 817-578-8588 or visit www.bellarosaconsignmentgallery.com. *(Color photo featured in front section of book.)*

Cactus Flower

Step inside the Cactus Flower, 104 N. Houston St., and you might think you've happened into a quaint boutique in the Southwest. Owner Debra Place opened her charming shop in 1994 and loves the definite flair she has added to Granbury's shopping experience. Cactus Flower started with a vacation to California with Debra's husband Gordon. On their return trip, they stopped at a little shop in Gallup, N.M., to buy turquoise earrings, and ended up taking some of the designer's jewelry home to sell. Debra began to visit trade shows and eventually opened her own store. She focuses on quality, affordable, casual wear and jewelry for women who want to dress for success with clothes that are timeless and comfortable. A few of her favorite lines are Focus and Multiples—all casual, classy clothes that go anywhere, anytime. You'll also find a fascinating collection of Southwestern treasures and home décor including handmade pottery, beautiful rugs and unique furniture. Call 817-573-7725.

PIZAZZ CONSIGNMENT BOUTIQUE

Put a little "pizazz" in your wardrobe at a fraction of the cost of retail. Pizazz Consignment Boutique, 1372 E. Hwy. 377, will become your favorite place to shop for designer clothing, jewelry and home décor at incredible resale prices. Owners Sally Davis and Kathi Roper met at a furniture consignment store and soon became great friends with a shared passion for fashion and design. Operating Pizazz has been a dream come true for the two friends … and for the ladies of Granbury. The store is a beautiful, friendly place to shop; customers say they can hardly believe it is resale! They comment, "Consignment stores have definitely changed. No longer are ladies embarrassed to say, 'I bought it resale,' especially if it is from a high-end resale boutique like Pizazz." Many customers become regulars, and great friends, and some even pitch in to help when Sally and Kathi are really busy." Visit www.pizazzconsignment.com or call 817-579-6777.

Furniture & Interior Décor and Design

Look for the sophisticated green and white awning over the window and the angel on the sign, and you're "almost in heaven." When Linda Preston moved back to Granbury after a 17-year absence, she named her store very appropriately. "I have always loved the town square," she admits, "so a business in one of these historic buildings was a dream come true." Actually, her grandparents once owned a grocery on Granbury's square, a place Linda happily spent many summer afternoons in her youth. She opened Almost Heaven, 118 N. Houston St., in 1980, and has seen it evolve into one of the town's most loved and respected boutiques. Linda's talent is without a doubt buying and merchandising, as evidenced by the clever displays and constantly changing inventory. From markets in Atlanta, New York,

Los Angeles and Dallas, she finds unique home décor and gifts. You'll love the remarkable selection of lighting and elegant tabletop décor, frames and photo albums, and unusual outdoor and garden elements. Visit www.almost-heaven.com or call 817-573-1591.

WAGON YARD

Imagine the year 1906 in a small country community, when townspeople would drive in from the outlying rural areas in their horse-drawn wagons. A stone building was constructed as a "wagon yard" where they would gather for activities around the Granbury square. Through the years, the historic building at 213 N. Crockett St., also served as a feed store, a restaurant and a photography studio. During the 1950s, a wing was added to the original structure, expanding it to almost 9,000 square feet.

Ray King moved his business into the interesting old "wagon yard" in 1977 to house his antiques and collectibles. The business evolved from an antique store to a remarkable collection of upscale furniture, lighting and home furnishings that complement all styles. The King family now operates the Wagon Yard, and they are just as committed to outstanding service, distinctive style and reasonable prices.

You will find such a large variety of styles here, from antiques and rustic Western and Old World to contemporary, traditional and French country. Locals love the store and always find just what they need, but visiting customers and designers travel from across the country for the unique lighting, beautiful art and outstanding furniture. You can even see a tin ceiling displayed before you order. From gorgeous ornate iron beds to antler chandeliers or carved candelabras and fireplace accessories, there are treasures for every room of your home. We loved the grand selection of weathervanes—airplanes, horses, boats, eagles and even golfers. And, for the game room, you'll find interesting signs, and a music collection that includes artists from the 1940s to the 1980s such as Dean Martin, Glenn Miller, Marty Robbins, Louis Armstrong and Patsy Cline. The Wagon Yard is an incredible store, filled with exceptional merchandise. Visit www.wagonyard.com or call 817-573-5321.

Furniture & Decorating

Pat Mahlen believes, "The way you decorate your living space can make the difference between a house and a home." Pat has been putting that philosophy into practice since 2003 when she bought Lane's Furniture & Decorating, 616 Fall Creek Hwy. in Granbury. Lane's is a beautiful showroom filled with vignettes of furniture, art and accessories from contemporary to traditional or transitional. You'll love the casual elegance and inspiration of color throughout the showroom. Of course, Pat's favorite part of her business is meeting with clients in their homes and helping them create their own signature looks. Pat offers this in-home design service throughout the DFW area, and her initial in-home visit is complimentary. Whether you just want to "update" your "outdated" draperies, or need someone to help you move things around for a new look, Pat will definitely make your home a special and beautiful place. Visit www.lanesfurniituregranbury.com and call 817-326-6203.

"We Handle Cowboy Equipment"

It's 100-percent "Cowboy-Owned-and-Operated!" The Cowboy Marketplace, 4170 E. Hwy. 377 is 10,000-square-feet of unique, Western and "cowboy" treasures. Owner Bennie Henson spent most of his youth in the rodeo. He turned pro in 1968 and traveled the United States and Canada for the PRCA as a bull rider and rodeo clown. (Guess you could say he's the real thing!) Bennie owned a home décor store/art gallery in Abilene before moving to Granbury in 1987. While preparing to open his other business, the Downtown Store, he met his wife Debbie. It was "love at first sight," he says. The couple opened the Cowboy Marketplace in 1991, and garnered a reputation for quality home furnishings and Western art. It's the perfect place to find home furnishings and collectibles with a true touch of the Old West—everything from hides and horns to cast iron cookware and turquoise jewelry. Out back, you'll find the 377 R.V. Park where there's even a "horse motel." Call 817-579-1315 or visit www. cowboy-marketplace.com. *(See related story on page 33.)*

ACCENTS II

Located at 440 Pearl St., Accents II sits just across from Granbury's new public beach and only three blocks from the town's famous, historic square. Accents II opened in 1999, and its loyal customers have been buying wonderful gifts, furniture and home décor from many of the same smiling, service-oriented staff members ever since. Owner Betsy Harty admits that her long-time employees and friends are a key to the store's success. Accents II is always loaded with new, carefully selected and artfully displayed merchandise. Candles, pottery, and kitchen items are a special focus and direct connections with furniture and textile manufacturers enhance Accents' ability to offer exceptional value and great selection.

Add its bridal and baby registry to the mix, and it's a winning combination. For more information, call 817-579-6076 or visit www.accents-home.com. And be sure to stop by Accents' other locations in Burleson and Cleburne … you'll be so glad you did!

the

Pan
Handle

a gourmet tool shop

Heather Cleveland took the original Chevrolet dealership in Granbury and transformed it into a bright, creatively decorated gourmet kitchen store. She calls it a "gourmet tool shop." The Pan Handle, 106 N. Crockett St., is a fantastic place for chefs of all abilities to find top-of-the-line tools that make the kitchen a fun place to work and play. And, the building itself has such a fascinating history and atmosphere. It is located in the showroom of the dealership and the front wall still has the garage door that enabled them to bring vehicles in and out.

Heather started this business right out of college in 1993. Although her educational background was in photography and art history, she had in-depth experience working retail. "I grew up in a 'gourmet' household with a fabulous cook for a mom," says Heather, "so it all seemed like a natural fit." Customers love her wonderful selection of high-end kitchen equipment, cookware, bakeware, textiles, ceramics, cutlery, coffees and specialty foods. The complete array of kitchen specialties includes state-of-the-art mixers, coffee makers, blenders and food processors. You will love browsing through the great selection of cookbooks from "Food Network" and across the United States. The Pan Handle offers special services like a bridal registry, and custom gift baskets and gift wrapping for every occasion. It is also well known for its exceptional wine and cooking classes taught by local chefs. Whether you're looking for a piece of Le Creuset cookware, a Kitchen Aid or just a pound of "Cowboy Java Brew" gourmet coffee, you'll find it here! You can also drop off your knives for sharpening, try the latest coffee beans or even swap a recipe! Call 817-579-1518 or visit www.thepanhandle.com.

Cindy Hyde loves Western and rustic home décor and furnishings! With just one visit to her store, you're sure to be inspired to add a little Lone Star luxury to your home. Dakota's Kabin, 202 N. Houston St., is located on the square in a historic building (circa 1893) that once served Granbury as a feed store. Locals were often found sitting around playing cards. You can even see the telltale signs of their visits by the many cigarette burns in the original wood floors. Since 1998, Cindy has assembled a remarkable selection of inventory as well as a stellar staff that is committed to offering only the best possible service. You'll find affordable Western décor from designers like Montana Silversmiths and Triple Creek. You will also find women and men's apparel by Cowgirl Tuff and Cinch Jeans as well as boots and shoes from Ariat and Corral Boots. Make sure to check out the store's special events like Christmas in July and the Pajama Party in December, both marked by great fun and even greater savings. Call 817-579-0275 or visit www.dakotaskabin.com. *(See related story on page 25.)*

DOWNTOWN STORE
ON THE SQUARE

Step inside the Downtown Store, 111 E. Bridge St. on the square in downtown Granbury, and you'll find exactly what you would imagine a small-town store would have been like 100 years ago. Old-fashioned candy displays entice young and old alike and gourmet foods from Texas, line the shelves. There is something for everyone. Kids love the aisles of favorite old-fashioned toys and games. Moms love the selection of unique kitchen gadgets and home décor, and everyone loves finding a great gift such as a beautiful piece of jewelry, an enchanting wind chime or cuddly baby items. You'll find a large selection of Texas and Granbury T-shirts and souvenirs and fine collectibles from Franz, Clayworks, and Madame Alexander Dolls. Owners Bennie and Debbie Henson share their time between this store and the Cowboy Marketplace, a great store for Western home décor and cowboy collectibles. For more information, call 817-579-1809. *(See related story on page 30.)*

Pamela & Co.

Pamela Padget is a true renaissance woman. In addition to being a devoted wife, mother and grandmother, she is a licensed professional counselor—who works with her husband, Dr. Larry Padget, family physician—real estate broker, author, shop owner and overall inspiration to women everywhere. It's that same inspiration and drive that she brings to her shop, Pamela & Co.

This girly, funky, hot pink sanctuary is located at 102 N. Houston St. on Granbury's historic downtown square. It's a colorful shop with a colorful history. Notorious bank robbers Bonnie and Clyde once used the space as a hideout, but today, Pamela has highlighted the building's softer side. "I wanted to have a store that excited all five senses with a love of history," she says. Pamela pays tribute to her infamous dad, Billie Sol Estes, in the book, "King of the Weeler Deelers." And, has now authored another book, "Until Your Fairy Godmother Arrives."

Pamela & Co. offers a delicious assortment of shop-made fudge. In addition to all this, you'll love browsing through beautiful antiques, fun jewelry, women and girl's clothing, and fabulous gifts while tasting salsa, dips and chipoltes. "You won't see another store like it," promises Pamela, "at least not til pigs fly!" It's a must-see on your Lady's Day Out! Call 817-579-8114 or visit www.pamelaandco.com. *(Color photo featured in front section of book.)*

Filled with beautiful gifts and fabulous home décor, St. Helen's gift boutique continues to earn rave reviews for its incredible ambience and fine selections. It is located at 135 E. Pearl St. in downtown Granbury in a wonderfully restored limestone building that has held several businesses through the years. In fact, it is named the St. Helen's Building for John St. Helen, a local legend who tended bar in its days as a saloon. Today, mother-and-daughter-team, Rita and Melissa Scott, fill the two-story space with an incredible selection of fine treasures for every room, occasion and season. We loved the beautiful selection of fragrances, candles and bath and body products by Niven Morgan, Lollia and Pre de Provénce. They also carry an eclectic collection of jewelry, handbags and accessories. During the holidays, the store is full of Christmas magic, featuring beautiful Old World ornaments. Visit www.sthelenstx.com or call 817-573-8388.

Enjoy leisurely walks through the beautifully landscaped gardens, cool dips in the flagstone pool or peaceful moments on the balcony overlooking the lake. Then retire to lovely rooms filled with fine European furnishings and luxurious bedding in Granbury's premier lakefront bed and breakfast. Owners Cathy Casey and Jim Leitch purchased and renovated the historic, 1880 Doyle House, in 2003. It was named for Dr. John Doyle, a Confederate Civil War surgeon who settled in Granbury after the war. It is now the extraordinary Inn on Lake Granbury, 205 W.

Doyle St., a perfect retreat for a romantic weekend. There are 13 guestrooms or suites with private baths, some with balconies or porches, jetted tubs and heated bathroom floors. Guests are served a full breakfast each morning and appetizers and beverages in the afternoons. Enjoy a weekend of casual elegance and luxurious comfort at The Inn on Lake Granbury. Call 817-573-0046 or visit www.innonlakegranbury.com.

Plantation Inn

ON THE LAKE•GRANBURY

With views of beautiful Lake Granbury and the stately courthouse, the historic Plantation Inn, 1451 E. Pearl St., is the perfect place to enjoy a weekend in this charming Texas town. You will feel almost lost in time and be treated like family by owners Dutch and Brenda Wilkinson. "You'll come to the hotel as a guest, but leave as a friend," they say. All 53 rooms open to the outside to luxurious greenery and the fragrance of Knock Out roses and magnolia trees. The white columns and wide portico lend an Old South ambiance to the hotel, which continues inside with soft leather wing backs and fine antiques. There is a courtyard with a pool, a children's wading pool, and charcoal grills. The best part of your stay, however, may be the delicious Southern breakfasts served each morning. And, to take advantage of all that Granbury has to offer, hop aboard the old-fashioned trolley for a ride to the historic square. Visit www.plantationinngranbury.com or call 817-573-8846. *(See related story page 21.)*

Built of hand-hewn native stone in 1893 by David Lee Nutt, The Historic Nutt House Hotel occupies the original site of a mercantile store that was first constructed on logs. It was here that brothers Jesse and Jake Nutt (both blind from birth) operated their general mercantile on Granbury's town square. Lovingly restored to house seven luxury suites, The Historic Nutt House Hotel, 119 E. Bridge St., is a wonderful combination of history, romance and elegance. Guests can enjoy a full day of exciting shopping on the square, see a live musical or have dinner in one of Granbury's delectable restaurants. Then treat yourself to a relaxing soak in an antique tub, slip into a comfy bathrobe and cozy down into luxury linens for the night. Historical ambiance from beautiful, period antiques coupled with modern services like free Wi-Fi and on-site massage therapy will make your stay memorable. Call 817-279-1207 or visit www.nutt-hotel.com. *(See related story on page 22.)*

Pearl Street Station
A Cajun & Bar-B-2 Eatery

Laissez les bons temps rouler! For the Cajun impaired that's "Let the Good Times Roll!" No one does this better than David and Kay Moore. Pearl Street Station is a Cajun and Bar-B-Q Eatery—located in a 1933 Sinclair gas station at 120 W. Pearl St., just off Granbury's historic square. Kay grew up on her grandparents' farm and began cooking at the age of five. "My Grandma Mattie was an excellent cook, and I've inherited her love of food," she says. "Her recipe for Crispy Corn Salad is one of our top sellers for catering." Everything on the menu is delicious, from fresh salads and sandwiches—our favorite is the Turkey with Lemon Dill Sauce—to heartier fare like Blackened Catfish and Cajun Grilled Shrimp. And, whether you're planning a Hawaiian Luau, a Western BBQ or a Cajun Fais do-do, the Moore's will make it memorable. They even put on a "Shotgun Wedding," complete with licensed minister, gunslingers for witnesses and country music. Visit www.pearlststationgranbury.com or call 817-579-7233.

Line Camp Steakhouse

If you've got a hankerin' for a real ranch steak and good ole Texas hospitality, we've got just the place for you!! The Line Camp Steakhouse, 4610 Shaw Rd., is a rare find, voted one of the top steakhouses in the state by *Texas Monthly* magazine. The family-run, family-friendly steakhouse is located a few miles from Granbury in the country setting of Tolar that might have been a perfect "line camp" for the cowboys of old. Before there were barbed-wire fences, there were "line camps" built just along the borders of the range, where, at the end of the day, the cowboys would gather for dinner and kick back by the campfire to sip a little whiskey and tell the tallest tales.

The Wienecke family (Wayne and Laurie, and children Landri, Wesley, Wyatt and Loryn) thought it was the perfect name for their authentic, Texas steakhouse, because like the camp lines of old, it is a place where customers can kick back, enjoy delicious food and drinks with friends and family and escape to a simpler time. Wayne says, "We used to travel with friends all the way to Buffalo Gap, Texas, to eat at a favorite steakhouse. We finally decided to try it ourselves. We entered the Texas Steak Cook-Off in Hico, Texas, with a promise that if we placed in the top three we would open our own steakhouse. We came in second! We drew our plans on a napkin, built the Line Camp and started grilling steaks."

One visit and you won't be able to forget the incredible flat iron steaks cooked over pecan wood and served with garlic butter, huge dressed baked potatoes, sautéed vegetables, homemade yeast rolls and scrumptious desserts. Occasionally, they even have that old-time favorite—Dr. Pepper Cake. The Line Camp has an enormous "backyard" complete with a cantina, stage and tables that can be reserved for private parties. Visit www.linecampsteakhouse.com or call 254-835-4459.

Featuring old-family recipes passed down throughout generations by their extraordinary West Texas grandmothers, the Vinyard family enterprise decorates the Texas landscape with a smattering of home-cooking restaurant concepts including Bubba's Cooks Country and Sweetie Pie's Ribeyes. Company founders and restaurant visionaries, Paul and his late wife, Mary Beth ventured into the highly competitive Dallas restaurant market with the 1981 opening of Bubba's in the chic University Park neighborhood of Dallas, in the heart of Snider Plaza, located close to S.M.U. The family opened the first Babe's Chicken Dinner House in 1993, located in Roanoke, followed by a second Babe's location in Garland in 1994.

Today, the family-owned-and-operated restaurant company features nine different and unique Babe's locations, as well as the original Bubba's, and including their new steakhouse venture, Sweetie Pies nestled in old downtown Decatur. Today Paul runs the business with his son Joel and daughter Tiffany at his side. Tiffany has been instrumental in the development of the companies flourishing catering venture. Joel and his sister continue to take on more and more of the responsibilities of running and operating a successful restaurant.

The Granbury Babe's, located at 114 W. Pearl St., sits on the outskirts of the historic downtown Granbury square, surrounded by shops and several B&B's, waiting to become your favorite place for great home-cooking, family-gatherings, and get-togethers with old friends. Featuring fried chicken and several other family recipes reminiscent of Sunday afternoons at Grandma's, Babe's is prepared to take you down memory lane. Meals are served family style with heaping platters of fried chicken, chicken fried steak, fried farm-raised catfish, hickory smoked chicken, chicken tenders, and Momma Jo's pot roast, and plentiful, steaming bowls of fluffy, buttery mashed potatoes, made-from-scratch gravy, corn, green beans and hot homemade biscuits that melt in your mouth. The late Mary Beth was often fond of telling folks "We cook everything in small batches, over and over. Our biscuits are made one little old pan at a time."

The Vinyard family strives to make each-and-every patron feel like they are eating at their grandmother's. Continuing to garner customer applause, Babe's has been featured on the "Food Network" and *Southern Living* magazine has also touted Babe's Chicken Dinner House as one of its favorites. You'll find the atmosphere casual, family friendly, fun and finger-lick'n good. For the hours they're open, as well as information about their other locations, visit www.babeschicken.com. If you're interested in Babe's catering your next event, call 817-573-9777. Come and experience Babe's Granbury!

Salons, Spas & Indulgence

BLUSHES

Established in 1983, Blushes is the oldest Salon/Spa in Granbury and was originally a dream of a fifteen-year-old girl, Jeanne, who has always been passionate about skin care. Mary, Jeanne's Mother was just as passionate about quality service that she felt was lacking in the salon industry in Granbury. So, together they set out to create an extraordinary dream for themselves and ultimately for their clients—doing all they could to make guests feel relaxed and beautiful.

Because of this dedication to exceptional service Blushes, 5464 Acton Hwy., has been featured in nine magazines, on *Good Morning Texas* and was honored by *The Ellen DeGeneres Show* when they were selected to style hair for the ladies on the "Road to Ellen" segment. With Jeanne's involvement the event was a huge success!

Of course, none of this would be possible without the wonderful clients and the dedication of all the professionals at Blushes. "This is not only business but this belongs to all of us." Jeanne says, "Blushes is a sanctuary, a place of serenity away from all the chaos and stress in our daily lives…"

Blushes offers all salon services for hair and nails, as well as pedicure treatments, facials, massages, body treatments, permanent make-up, waxing and products for detoxification and nutrition.

Jeanne, now with her own daughter, has taken the reins and her dream has come true. As the owner of Blushes, she is creating her own vision of an extraordinary salon/spa that adds amazing value to clients and community. For more information, call 817-326-0197 or visit www.blushessalon.com.

HEAD 2 TOE
Spa
Salon

Audrie Tibljas worked hard as a massage therapist in her one-room suite for a few years, before deciding to expand into a luxury spa and salon. Head 2 Toe is located at 1459 N. Plaza Dr. in Granbury, across from Kroger. The beautiful space is an eclectic combination of colors and textures; exotic plum purple with zebra accents, soothing mint green massage rooms and billowing silk-draped ceilings. One of its most popular services is the "couples' massage." Rose petals are scattered over the sheets, the lights are dimmed, and the couple enjoys a wine spritzer while sharing an exhilarating massage. The Spa also hosts a women's night out with a large variety of spa services available like facials, bodywraps, haircare, airbrush tanning and much more. Head 2 Toe also carries a great selection of accessories and gifts in the salon boutique. A wonderful experience in a beautiful place! Call 817-579-8778.

Sport Shops

Okay ladies, we've found the perfect place to stash your man on your Lady's Day Out in Granbury! He'll be perfectly happy to leave you alone for hours—and both will appreciate that! Doug's Sports House, 120 N. Crockett St., is a complete "man cave," with a 42" flat-screen television that always has the game on. Owners Doug and Connie Knippa have quite a collection that will interest any man, including NASCAR memorabilia, hunting and fishing gear, golfing items and biker gear. It is definitely a man's dream store. Although Doug bleeds "burnt orange" (for Texas Longhorns), he carries great collegiate items from other teams. And, during the big games, guys chow down on hot dogs and sports drinks. Doug says, "My store is a 'two-fer.' It's a great place for the guys to rest while the gals shop and the guys usually find something they just have to have here." Visit www.dougssportshouse.com or call 682-936-2729.

HOUSTON ST. MERCANTILE

With its bright red awning, gleaming hardwood floors and potted flowers at the front door, the charming little cottage at 126 N. Houston St. makes an absolutely perfect quilt shop. The old-fashioned atmosphere, beautiful displays and remarkable fabrics and quilting supplies have helped Houston St. Mercantile become one of Granbury's most beloved venues.

Owner Glenda Westbrook left the corporate world of insurance in 1989 to open a gift shop that specialized in stained glass art, wooden furniture, unusual handmade gifts and delightful collectibles. She slowly became interested in fabrics and the art of quilting. That hobby grew and transformed her endearing store into one of the most versatile quilt shops in the Metroplex.

Even if you've never quilted before, you must see the beautiful creations and wonderful selections of fabrics and accessories displayed throughout the store. There are more than 4,000 bolts of fabrics (flannels, woven brushed cottons, batiks and others) from well-known designers like Moda, Hoffman, Kaufman, RJR, Maywood and more. Glenda has fabulous quilts displayed, along with patterns (some which can only be found at Houston's) and supplies to create the same patterns. In fact, you can buy the entire quilt in a package, or join the "block of the month" for a prepackaged supply of everything you'll need to build your quilt "one block at a time."

Glenda and her quilt-savvy staff are eager to help new quilters and offer classes to get you started or help you advance your skills. Experienced quilters will find Houston's specialty bees enticing. Houston St. Mercantile is also an authorized Baby Lock machine dealer. Call 817-279-0425 or visit www.houstonstmercantile.com.

Discover
Grapevine

Great things just have to come out of a town with a name like Grapevine! It's such a wonderful place to visit, and we just know it will become one of your favorite get-a-ways. We have enjoyed every single minute of discovering this great little north Texas town, and have so many exciting things to share. We experienced the almost forgotten exhilaration of an old-fashioned train ride, found wonderful pieces of art, tapped our toes at the Opry and found way too many treasures we just could not leave behind. And holidays in Grapevine have to be experienced to be believed! Historic Grapevine, with its wonderful collection of shops, restaurants, galleries and entertainment venues is an outstanding vacation destination. There are delightful restaurants, cafés and tearooms, and wine tasting rooms. There are also wonderful outdoor recreational activities and exciting festivals and special events throughout the year.

Grapevine is a haven for local artists and art lovers. You can take the nine-stop Grapevine arts trail through downtown to see many of the artists demonstrate their work. Or, hop aboard a vintage train for a themed rail adventure and end the evening at the famed Palace Theatre where country music is still king.

Tah-Wah-Karro Creek to Grapevine

Grapevine is actually the oldest settlement in Tarrant County, originating in 1844 under the Lone Star Flag—before Texas even became part of the United States. The settlement was founded that year when General Sam Houston and Republic of Texas

Commissioners camped at Tah-Wah-Karro Creek (also known as Grape Vine Springs) to meet with leaders of the Indian nations. A peace treaty was signed, at that time ushering in the settlement by homesteaders and pioneers, and they named their community Grapevine, after the tart, wild Mustang grapes that blanketed the area around Grape Vine Prairie and Grape Vine Springs. Prosperity "steamed" into Grapevine in 1888 with the arrival of the St. Louis Southwestern Railroad (otherwise known as the Cotton Belt Railroad), and the town grew steadily through the decades. Progress increased quite a bit with the development of the Dallas/Ft. Worth International Airport in the 1970s, and then once again found an outlet for tremendous growth in the wine business. The Texas Wine and Grape Growers Association moved to Grapevine in 1990 and a delicious wine industry began to define this little town with the perfect "wine" name. Attention to Grapevine as an up-and-coming wine town also made it a popular destination for new businesses, and it began to draw new families and retirees. It's a town with a rich history and a very promising (and delicious) future!

Shop and Dine Grapevine

Even the most seasoned shopper will be impressed with the abundance of exciting opportunities in Grapevine. From upscale and trendy to down-home and cozy restaurants and boutiques, there is an extraordinary selection of unique ideas, gifts and sustenance that will keep you busy for days. Plan to spend enough time in Grapevine to really get to know the town and enjoy everything that makes it such a fabulous little Texas treasure.

You will fall in love with Grapevine's historical downtown district. Main Street has earned its spot on the National Register of Historic Places and is full of beautiful buildings that have been lovingly restored to both preserve their historical significance and function as a vibrant part of Grapevine's future. The past meets the present in this family-friendly entertainment environment filled with great antique stores, wonderful clothing boutiques, bead shops, art galleries and even a store dedicated to nothing but chocolate! Be sure to wander into **Bermuda Gold & Silver** on Main Street. Now a fabulous jewelry store filled with beautiful baubles and beads; it was once a bank that was actually robbed by members of Bonnie and Clyde's Barrow Gang. Another business on the square that has been transformed with time is Willhoite's Restaurant. Built in 1914 as a dry goods store, it later became the town's first gas station. You'll still see the vintage gas pumps, but the site is now known for its delicious buffet, and lively weekend musical entertainment. You'll say, **Ooh La La**! to fabulous clothing and fun accessories in this charming boutique and feel as though you've crossed the seas to merry England at the **British Emporium**.

Walk the entire downtown, discovering the goodies of Grapevine and getting to know the people. From wonderful home décor and fine art to a favorite candle, a "have-to" handbag or a beautiful embroidery pattern, you're sure to find something special as a memento of your visit. When you need a little break, and a place to share your finds, stop in at one of the delightful cafés, and enjoy a delicious lunch and a sweet treat.

Grapevine is also famous for having one of the largest destination malls in the southwestern United States. Grapevine Mills is 1.6-million-square-feet of shopping, dining and entertainment fun. There is free transportation from many hotels to historic Main Street and Grapevine Mills Mall, so it's easy to get around.

Grapevine's De"Vine" Wine Experience

This aptly named town is famous for its fruit-of-the-vine experience. In fact, it is always advertised with a cluster of purple grapes by its name. With nine tasting rooms and a vineyard in town, Grapevine has become a popular destination for "oenophiles" or wine collectors and enthusiasts. You can leisurely enjoy a day or night of wine tasting, find unique wine accessories and even put your own label on a favorite bottle of vino. It's a wine lover's perfect weekend getaway.

The city really lives up to its name in the fall, which is harvest season. Wine lovers and fun-seekers head to Grapevine during the fall for the largest wine festival in the southwest. **GrapeFest** is held each year in September and is the largest consumer-judged wine competition in the nation. Raise your glass of award-winning wine and enjoy delicious culinary treats in historic downtown. For more fun, kick your shoes off and actually be part of the winemaking process at **GrapeStomp**. It's great, messy fun, and the winner goes home with the coveted "Purple Foot Award!" Be sure to stop by **Off the Vine** and pick up a bottle or two to take home.

All Aboard the Grapevine Vintage Railroad

If you've never had the chance to experience the clack of wheels on the rail or feel the sway of a train car, board the Grapevine Vintage Railroad. It's more than a train ride; it's an experience you will never forget. The station is serviced by two vintage locomotives: Puffy the 1896 steam locomotive and a GP-7 diesel locomotive. Also known as the Cotton Belt Railroad, the vintage trains travel from Grapevine to the Ft. Worth Stockyards several days a week and offer themed adventure for every age. You can hop on board the Jazz Wine Train or even pop the question on the Sweetheart Express. "Thomas the Tank Engine" rolls into Grapevine during the spring and becomes a life-size toy for children (of all ages) who love trains. Oh, and don't listen to nay-sayers who may tell you that it's sometimes "unsafe" to ride the rail from Grapevine. They must have been onboard during one of the famous "Great Train Robberies," when desperate outlaws stage a great show of Wild West fun!

Every December, the train becomes the famous North Pole Express, filled with pajama-clad youngsters who receive special gifts from Santa, who has hitched a ride to the Christmas Village. Once there the North Pole General Store offers free ornament-making, pictures with Santa and great shopping.

All I Want For Christmas!

All we want for Christmas is to visit Grapevine during the holidays. It is such an incredible experience that the town has been named The Christmas Capital of Texas! Historic downtown Grapevine is decorated top to bottom with millions of lights, shiny decorations and even snow! The entire town (and many visiting friends) gather at the Town Square Gazebo right before Thanksgiving each November to celebrate the beginning of the holiday season as a switch gets flipped to ignite thousands and thousands of glittering lights.

It is said that holiday shoppers have more gift options than any place south of the North Pole; strolling entertainers are dressed in period Christmas costumes; decorated horse-drawn carriages clip-clop through the tinseled streets and Santa has the best seat in town! There is even a Twinkle Light Boat Parade on Lake Grapevine, a Lone Star Christmas at the Gaylord Texan Resort, a dazzling Snow Land at the Great Wolf Lodge and the Grapevine Opry puts on its most elaborate and special show of the year during Christmas at the grand Palace Theatre. Grapevine is a winter wonderland during this magical time of the year. Don't miss it!!

Toe Tapping Entertainment in Grapevine

Grapevine is extremely proud to have the brilliantly renovated Palace Arts Center, which includes the fully restored Palace and Lancaster Theaters. The Palace Theatre, which was built in 1940 is home to the wonderful **Grapevine Opry**, a Grapevine tradition for more than 70 years. When the Palace opened in 1940, it was to Olivia de Haviland's performance in *My Love Came Back*. It operated as a first-run movie theater until it closed 1973, then reopened in 1975, and closed again in 1983. The Grapevine Opry opened at the Palace Theatre again in 1984 with a performance by seven-year-old LeAnn Rimes, and thanks to community leaders and dedicated patrons, country music is still alive and king here today. The Opry presents a live country showcase each weekend, with special entertainment during the holidays. You'll love shows like God & Country, Makin'Time with Patsy Cline, Fabulous Fifties Jukebox, Elvis Day at the Grapevine Opry and a tribute to George Strait.

Grapevine Opry may be small, but the performances are "Texas big!" It showcases the best up-and-coming talent from around the country with wildly popular country music and spontaneous humor to packed houses of fans who come back time after time. Through the years audiences have been thrilled to see performers like Willie Nelson, the Judds, Jimmy Dean, LeAnn Rimes, Keith Anderson and Miranda Lambert.

As you can see by our experiences in Grapevine, we fell in love with this amazing little up-and-coming town. It radiates that real small-town America feeling, but is shining itself up to contend with larger sister cities as an incredible vacation destination. With its easy access to the entire Metroplex and just minutes from DFW International Airport, it's pretty easy to find and navigate. We left Grapevine with an invitation from the friendly locals and business owners to our readers: "Come visit; we're expecting you anytime!!!"

Call the City of Grapevine Convention and Visitor's Bureau at 817-410-3578, 800-457-6338 or visit www.GrapevineTexasUSA.com, for more information.

Grapevine
Fairs Festivals & Fun

January
- First Friday Film Series
- Grapevine Opry at the Palace Theatre

February
- First Friday Film Series
- Grapevine Vintage Railroad
- Grapevine Opry at the Palace Theatre
- Sweetheart Express Wine Train
- Sweetheart Wine Trail

March
- First Friday Film Series
- Grapevine Vintage Railroad
- Grapevine Opry at the Palace Theatre
- ChocolateFest
- Day Out With Thomas

April
- First Friday Film Series
- Grapevine Market
- Farmers Market
- Grapevine Vintage Railroad
- Grapevine Opry at the Palace Theatre
- Day Out With Thomas
- New Vintage Wine & Gallery Trail
- New Vintage Jazz Wine Trains
- Spring into Nash Farm

May
- First Friday Film Series
- Grapevine Market
- Farmers Market
- Grapevine Vintage Railroad
- Great Train Robberies
- Grapevine Opry at the Palace Theatre
- Main Street Days
- SummerBlast

June
- First Friday Film Series
- Grapevine Market
- Farmers Market
- Grapevine Vintage Railroad
- Grapevine Opry at the Palace Theatre

July
- First Friday Film Series
- Grapevine Market
- Farmers Market
- Grapevine Vintage Railroad
- Grapevine Opry at the Palace Theatre
- July 4th Fireworks Extravaganza over Lake Grapevine
- Red, Whites and You Wine Trail

August

First Friday Film Series
Grapevine Market
Farmers Market
Grapevine Vintage Railroad
Grapevine Opry at the Palace
  Theatre
Summer Wine Train

September

First Friday Film Series
Grapevine Market
Farmers Market
Grapevine Vintage Railroad
Great Train Robberies
Grapevine Opry at the Palace
  Theatre
SummerBlast
GrapeFest

October

First Friday Film Series
Grapevine Market
Farmers Market
Grapevine Vintage Railroad
Grapevine Opry at the Palace
  Theatre
Butterfly Flutterby
Fall Round-Up at Nash Farm
Candlelight Tour of Homes
Hallo-Wine Trail

November

First Friday Film Series
Grapevine Vintage Railroad
Grapevine Opry at the Palace
  Theatre
North Pole Express®
Christmas on Main
Lone Star Christmas and Ice at
  the Gaylord Texas Resort
Light Show Spectacular
Carol of Lights

December

Grapevine Opry at the Palace
  Theatre
North Pole Express®
Christmas on Main
Lone Star Christmas and Ice at
  the Gaylord Texas Resort
Light Show Spectacular
Snow Land at Great Wolf
  Lodge
Parade of Lights
Twinkle Light Boat Parade
Christmas Musicals at the
  Palace Theatre
Family Christmas Movies at
  the Palace Theatre
Grapevine Opry Christmas
  Spectacular

Antiques

Gary Farina had a love for fine antiques that began long before he decided to open his store **Antique Revival**, located at 418 S. Main St. in the heart of historic downtown Grapevine. During his travels through Europe, he discovered many one-of-a-kind treasures and honed his knowledge of the antique business world. Unique inventory of furniture, both large and small, sets of china, religious artifacts and a vast selection of vintage jewelry make his store a must-see in downtown. It's the perfect place to find that one-of-a-kind gift.

After shopping it's time to relax. Step across the threshold into **Farina's Winery & Café** and the warm antique charm and ambience continue. Enjoy a glass of wine from the beautiful antique bar with its majestic mirror that dates back to the 1800s. Choose something delicious to eat from the Italian cuisine prepared daily. Gary has created an outstanding shopping and dining experience where friends meet. You owe it to yourself to stop in... Salut!

To get more information or to plan your special event, call Sally at 817-329-7882.

Attractions & Entertainment

It has been called, "One of the premier, live music shows in the nation!" The Grapevine Opry is located in the restored Palace Theater, 300 S. Main St. Originally built as a movie house in 1939, it was renamed Grapevine Opry during the late 1970s. Closed during the mid-1980s, the Grapevine Opry re-opened in 1987 and was renovated in 2001. Today, folks come from across the country to enjoy the theater's acclaimed band. Themed shows include 50s Rock 'n Roll, Gospel, Pop and Country Western. Producer, musician and bandleader Rocky Gribble has entertained crowds for four decades, and The Grapevine Opry has thrived under his leadership since 1987. Visit www.gvopry.com for information about the exciting performances that include a popular "Elvis" show, a patriotic 4th of July show and, of course, spectacular holiday entertainment. Call 817-481-8733. *(See related information on page 50.)*

Gather a few good friends and a favorite bottle of wine and learn to paint?!? Painting with a Twist, 203 E. Worth St., is definitely a novel idea in historic Grapevine, but one that is catching on quickly. Colleen Grant visited one of these art studios in New Orleans with her sister and loved it so much that she decided to buy the first franchise in Texas. Groups of friends can enjoy a glass (or two) of wine while they paint a picture step-by-step along with a local artist. "We offer the opportunity for people to engage the creative side of their brain," Colleen says. "Many come in and find out how enjoyable it is and come back again and again." She provides paint, canvas, brushes and a professional instructor. After an evening of creativity and camaraderie, everyone takes home a beautiful work of art and discovers a new-found talent! Get some girls together for that special event or come alone and join the fun—perfect for a girls' night out, or any reason. Call 817-328-8788 or visit www.paintingwithatwist.com/grapevine.

Garden Manor
Bed and Breakfast Inn

To her family and friends, Judy Dusek seemed to have it all. She was a successful single woman with a dream job in corporate America. So when she sold her home, resigned from her position and purchased a rundown home in Grapevine's historic district, they thought she had lost her mind! But Judy had a vision of getting out of the corporate rat race and opening a luxurious bed and breakfast where she could cater to her guests in a style reminiscent of her West

Texas upbringing. She renovated the home and turned it into Garden Manor Bed & Breakfast Inn, 205 E. College St. This elegant, Southern Georgia style home with sweeping verandas and lush gardens is a premier venue for outdoor weddings and corporate events. The house has high ceilings with the original doors, hardwood floors, and wood-paned windows. The four guest rooms have been designed with garden themes, reflecting the beautiful outdoor historic gardens. Guests have the convenience of free DSL and a flat-screen TV with DVD and cable. Each room has a private bathroom and access to the veranda. Call 817-424-9177 or visit www.gardenmanorbandb.com.

Residence Inn®
Marriott.

Start your day at the Residence Inn with a free hot breakfast buffet then get out and about Grapevine to its many exciting attractions. This lovely highrise hotel at 2020 State Hwy. 26 is just minutes away from the DFW Airport, just across the street from the Grapevine Mills Shopping Mall, and, for all of the anglers, right next to the Bass Pro Shop. Guests enjoy a complimentary shuttle to any attraction within five miles, highspeed Internet, and 27" flat screen televisions. A fully equipped kitchen with granite counters in each room make it perfect for extended business stays. The remarkable staff is extremely helpful and with a mission to help you experience the comfort of your home-away-from-home. End the day with a relaxing visit to the onsite Library Bar and Grill. Start to finish, it's a wonderful day at the Residence Inn. Visit www.marriott.com/DALGP or call 972-539-8989.

Let's Pretend
☕ *Tea Parties* 👑
Fairy Tale Fun and Girly Boutique
Children's Tea Parties Since 1993!

Holly Northcutt describes her charming business as "Fairy Tale Fun and Girly Boutique." From the moment her daughters, Addison and Brookie were born, she knew this would be the perfect business for her. Let's Pretend, 317 Jenkins St., is a little girl's Tea Room specializing in birthday parties. It's a fun, frilly place where princesses of all ages can pretend and shop for specialty items and accessories. Birthday parties are magical here, with Royal Tea Cupcakes, fancy dress up clothes and even a Royal Treatment Salon where party girls can be pampered. Let's Pretend has been part of Grapevine since 1993 and is one of the oldest businesses in historic downtown. It is especially known for the Princess Parades held during birthday parties and seasonal events like Breakfast with Cinderella, Miss Spider's Tea and the Nutcracker. Stop by, for "Cupcakes and Tea," and during the week, no reservations are needed. Call 817-421-6678 or visit www.letspretendteaparties.com.

Camping & RVing

It is described as "a secret oasis" in the middle of the DFW Metroplex—a beautiful place to escape the hustle and bustle and enjoy the pleasures of nature and wildlife. The Vineyards Campground & Cabins, 1501 N. Dooley St., is a peaceful retreat of wooded countryside and waterfront areas. Even though it feels remote, it is still close to popular shopping, restaurants and recreational opportunities.

First developed as a park by the U.S. Corp of Engineers in the early 1960s, the property was rebranded in 2006 by the City of Grapevine as a campground and RV park. Sitting on 52-acres next to a protected Cross Timbers forest, the lakeside property was opened as The Vineyards Campgrounds & Cabins. Developers envisioned a place where people could take pleasure in camping and 'unplug' from the world to enjoy the outdoors. In the fall of 2010, the City of Grapevine completed a $1.7 million renovation project that included upgrading sewer service, creating premium RV campsites, adding seven new cabins and a campstore.

You can choose from 12 rustic one- and two-bedroom cabins that have furnished kitchens, linens, HD TVs, and outdoor porches, with most overlooking a picnic table, fire circle and BBQ grill. What could be more fun than circling around the fire, roasting marshmallows and gazing at the bright Texas stars?

Campers can take advantage of the boat ramp, fishing pier, playground, lakeside beach area and a nature trail. A large pavilion features heating units, a large fire pit, BBQ grills, a horseshoe court and oversized group picnic tables, perfect for, family reunions, Scout troops, or *A Lady's Day* (or Night!) *Out.* There is absolutely no agenda, but there are attend-if-you-like events like ice cream socials, fireworks and free concerts. Visit www.vineyardscampground.com or call 888-329-8993.

Fashion & Accessories

When Dana Hardiman-Jobe opened her boutique at 340 S. Main St., she knew the perfect name for the unique

Azure Alley
A Fashion Forward Boutique

space—Azure Alley. The building was originally an alley between two historical buildings in downtown Grapevine, so the store is long and narrow... and very cozy. "Azure means 'clear blue skies,'" Dana explains, "and for me, Azure Blue is a symbol that with God, His blue sky is the limit." After years of dedicating herself to her family and her career in education and corporate America, Dana decided to do something just for herself. She returned to retail—a passion she first discovered as a teenager. She worked for four years managing a boutique before forging her own path and opening her shop. Azure

Alley offers fashions from designers like Daniel Rainn and Razzle Dazzle and footwear by Yellow Box and Corral Boots. Expect to walk into this fun boutique and be welcomed with a warm smile and possibly an eager wag from the resident mascot, Lily. Call 817-310-3499.

Willow Cottage is where 'Vintage Charm meets eclectic style—for all life's events.' Featuring whimsical gifts, home décor and trendy fashions for women and children. Original artwork lines the walls, and stunning jewelry—by both local and well-known designers—is on display. Owner Kathy Diamond has successfully blended her exceptional offerings with Grapevine's historical significance. Willow Cottage, at 326 S. Main St., retains the vintage charm of the 100-year-old building that once housed Grapevine's first general store. Numerous chandeliers illuminate the original brick walls while showcasing the flirty fashions and lovely home décor items.

Don't miss Grapevine Olive Oil Company (682-223-1592), owned by Rebecca Knop and located inside Willow Cottage, where you can find 40 flavored olive oils that can be sampled before you buy. It beautifully blends the charm of yesteryear with the French country look, as well as the style of today.

For more information, visit www.willowcottagegrapevine.com or call 817-310-0472.

One loyal customer from Arizona wrote, "You are my favorite store in ALL of Texas!," and that's a lot of territory to cover! Closet Treasures, 421 S. Main St. in historic Grapevine, has been a dream come true for friends Debbie and Lisa. They have combined their exuberance and creative energy to create a part upscale consignment "we want every woman to be able to own designer label clothing at a fraction of the cost," says Debbie, and part new designs with new fashions arriving weekly. Of course, you'll find more than fashions here. You might find a vintage necklace or beaded evening bag, a designer scarf or ball gown or even a new chandelier from the Czech Republic or a piece of Molinari Murano crystal art. It is a unique and clever mix of old and new, funky and fabulous, elegant and fun. Call 817-421-8525 or visit www.closettreasures.net.

ooh la la!

smart & sassy fashions

The name says it all! One visit to this swanky boutique and you'll understand why it was voted "Best of the Besbettcue in Grapevine, Colleyville and Southlake for four years, and "Best Specialty Boutique in Tarrant County" in 2010. Ooh La La, 408 S. Main St., is located in the heart of historic downtown Grapevine in the original M. Jenkins Tate Building, which is listed on the National Register of Historic Places. The fashionable boutique caters to women who want a classic, yet unique look and attitude, offering wonderful, trendy lines of clothing, jewelry, accessories and gifts.

Owner Sylvia Helton is described as a "firecracker", a savvy businesswoman with extraordinary style, and was born to own such a hugely successful store. She is a jewelry designer whose family has been in the retail business for three generations, so it's in her genes! She says, "After braving the corporate world for many years, I cane across an opportunity to get into the retail business and to follow in the family footsteps. Ooh La La was a dream-come-true!"

Sylvia's exuberance and creativity are evident throughout the store in both the great customer service and the clever displays of exclusive lines such as Mesmerize and Desigual from Spain. She also carries the wonderful, embroidered Miss Me Jeans, which sell out as fast as they come in, and the chic and fabulous painted sweaters and scarves by Adore. You will also love, love, love the accessories that make you look and feel great in your clothes, like SPANX, Yummie Tummie and the new Cleavage Coolers—a pretty little pillow you keep in the freezer and then tuck into the front of your bra for a burst of cold refreshment when needed. Ooh La La! Call 817-329-8686 or visit www.oohlalatx.com.

Even though Michelle Plawecki was born in Chicago, she has always been a "cowgirl" at heart. After living for a while in Veracruz, Mexico, she happily returned to the States as a teenager and settled in the Metroplex. A self-proclaimed fashionista and lover of all things Western, Michelle combined her two passions into one chic Grapevine store, Coyote Cowboy, 411 S. Main St. The building itself is a treat to explore. Originally a two-story structure, it has housed many local landmarks over the years—a telephone exchange, the Mabrey Drug Store, the Grapevine Sun and even Grapevine's City Hall (until 1997). You'll love Michelle's cool inventory

of men and women's clothing, boots and hats. Great items arrive all the time, so stop by often—you don't want to miss a thing. For more information, call 817-481-1315.

Tally ho! Be prepared to hear the Queen's English spoken as you browse British Emporium, one of the top British stores in America! Alexandra Evans and Sheela Kadam opened this charming, truly unique shop in 1992 so that they could share their favorite teas and groceries with their friends in Texas. Little did they know that they would create such a loyal following! Brits and Anglophiles from all over the Metroplex flock to this store to visit Great Britain right in the heart of historic Grapevine. Located at 140 N. Main St., British Emporium offers hard-to-find imported groceries, teas, teapots, china, clotted cream, scones, preserves, proper Cadbury's chocolate, souvenirs and gifts. Today the Emporium also carries imports from Australia, India and South Africa! You simply have to experience Alexandra and Sheela's British hospitality. They both are firm believers in giving back to the community and are famous for their charitable and special events. From car shows and comedy festivals to royal and Scottish celebrations, there's something for everyone. We think Her Majesty would approve! Visit www.british-emporium.com or call 817-421-2311.

Liz Hendricks and Nancy Rosol hope that the minute you walk through their front door you'll feel as though you are standing on "Holy Ground." Whether you stop by for coffee beans, a Christian book or gift, you will fall in love with Holy Grounds, 336 S. Main St. It is truly a unique coffee shop and boutique, located in the historic Farmer's Bank Building, which still has the original bank safe. (By the way, even though they didn't rob the bank, Bonnie and Clyde did stop by once!)

Liz and Nancy consider the store to be their 'mission field,' and have a prayer wall with prayer requests from customers. They pray over them every night, and hope that God's love is evident in the store and in their lives. "We heard a call to open this little 'beacon of light' in historic Grapevine in 2006," they say, "Within a few short months, the door was open, the coffee was grinding, and the people were coming!" People have continued to come through the years, making Holy Grounds one of their favorite places to buy gourmet coffee beans and shop for the perfect one-of-a-kind gift. It's amazing to see how much merchandise they fit into the old bank building— custom-made pillows, candle art, stone crosses, stuffed animals, framed hymns, T-shirts, and of course, Bibles, books and journals. You'll also find the most beautiful Christening gowns and baby

clothes, (which Liz and Nancy buy with their own grandbabies in mind.) You'll love the selection of more than 100 flavors of both regular and decaf coffee beans. Their most popular flavor— Snickerdoodle! Stop by Holy Grounds for a hot sample of coffee, and say hello to their dogs, Ken and Barbee—who are only in the store Weekdays, they get weekends off. Call 817-329-0298 or visit www.holygroundsshop.com.

FANCY THIS! As an international flight attendant for 38 years, Marcia Vanden Eykel had the opportunity to shop all over the world, and always "fancied" owning her own boutique. She says that God has been with her every step of the way in making that dream come true. Fancy This, 202 W. Wall St. in Grapevine, is located on a historical property that Marcia purchased from the original owners. She restored this small slice of heaven to its 1950s charm and patterned it after the boutiques she loved to visit in Europe—small but filled to the brim with endearing treasures. *Southern Lady* magazine recently listed it as a store not to miss. With just one visit, you'll understand why. You'll love browsing for

items such as Roundtop metal yard art, Music of the Spheres—which Marcia calls the Stradivarius of wind chimes and clean burning soy candles by Swan Creek. Visit www.fancythisatgrapevine.com or call 817-488-3014.

Interior Décor and Design

Owner Debbie Kellum credits two incredible women for her passion and success in the retail business: her mother who managed a specialty boutique and her first employer, proprietor of a clothing boutique in Hobbs, N.M. When Debbie decided to open Ashlins in 2001, in historic downtown Grapevine, she fell in love with the little house where Grapevine's Old Gun Shop had been for many years. And as much as Debbie loved the location; the locals loved Ashlins even more. The boutique grew from that small house into a larger property and finally into its current location at 413 S. Main St., site of the Old City Hall. Inside you'll find a European feel and an exclusive mix of items for you and your home, including antique reproductions, Italian pottery and home décor and gifts from designers like Jan Barboglio and Waxing Poetic. Be sure to check out the Old City Hall safe that is now the bargain room. Ashlins also caters to shopping groups, so call Debbie and she will put a unique shopping experience together for your group. Call 817-442-0400 or visit www.ashlins.com.

Home Decor

When Pandamonium first opened as a premier home décor boutique, it was in a 580-square-foot space. "It was always 'pandemonium' in such a small space," owner, Dee Anne Williford laughs. "Arriving products were frequently unpacked on the back porch in any type of weather!" Thankfully, those days are long gone. Today, this beautiful shop, located in Grapevine's historic district at 317 S. Main St., fills an important spot in the town's history. Built in 1945, its building once served as the Commissioners Court, holding all the county's court records, and has the cement vault and iron door to prove it! Now, beautiful vignettes of gorgeous

furniture pieces and stunning accessories fill the space and the only 'pandemonium' here is in the uproar of the clients' accolades. The design staff invites you to bring in pictures of your home décor projects and they can assist with your selections. Floral designers are on-hand several days a week for custom orders. Visit www.pandamoniumdecor.com or call 817-424-0705.

Bermuda Gold & Silver

In December 1932, the Grapevine Home Bank was robbed at gunpoint by members of Bonnie and Clyde's gang! But for the last three decades, the historic bank building at 404 S. Main St. has been filled with gold—jewelry that is. Since 1987, Bermuda Gold & Silver has been family-owned-and-operated. Debi Meek began working at the store in 1992 and became the owner in 2008. She renovated the beautiful old building, using original marble and interesting items from its past. She has even recreated a "teller's window" with a marble piece on loan from Julie Florence, whose dad and grandfather previously owned the building. The "Bermuda Gold & Silver Gang" as she refers to her staff are knowledgeable jewelry (and history!) experts who will make your visit an exciting experience. You'll find a spectacular selection of fine jewelry, watches and popular items such as Reflection Beads and Lampe Berger. Call 817-481-5115 or visit www.bermudagoldjewelry.com. *(Color photo featured in front section of book.)*

There are beads, beads and more beads, in every color, shape and size, but Beads on the Vine, 314 S. Main St., is much more than a bead shop. It is a remarkable place to buy custom designed jewelry, beaded belts, wonderful purses and more.

Owner Alice Bryant has always had a passion for creating jewelry. She worked in a fine jewelry store in Newbury Port, Mass., and then joined the corporate world for several years. Once in Grapevine, she and a friend started making fashion jewelry for family and friends, and she loved it so much that she quit her job and started working at what was then Buster's Beads. When the owner mentioned that she might want to sell, Alice bought it within the week! "It is exactly what I love doing," she says, "I love people, and I've met so many wonderful women who have brought great joy into my life. The store is a great place to work and shop—we all have so much fun here. I feel truly blessed!" Alice specializes in custom jewelry for weddings, formal or casual wear, and says that she especially loves working with brides because it's such a special time in their lives.

You'll find magnificent beads from around the world, sterling silver and fashion jewelry. You can even take a beading class any Saturday morning. Be sure to ask about the popular Troll Beads, unique creations inspired by mythology, astrology, fairy tales and nature. Made from sterling, gold, Italian Murano glass, pearls or precious stones, each bead tells a personal story. You can start a necklace or bracelet with just one bead and create your own design. For information call 817-416-7272 or visit www.beadsonvine.com.

Oh, and look for Abby, the fluffy pooch, in what else—a beaded collar!

Just one bite of their flaky croissants filled with almond cream, a butter Danish filled with vanilla bean cream cheese or a cranberry scone with fresh creamy butter, and you'll think you are a world away in a small French village. Fabien and Yasmine Goury, both originally from France, loved Grapevine the minute they visited, and knew it would be the perfect place for their French Bistro and Bakery. MainStreet Bistro and Bakery, 316 S. Main St., opened in 2000, and it didn't take long for everyone to discover their incredible French pastries and decadent desserts. The award-winning bakery is famous for its handcrafted breads, pastries and gourmet cuisine made by traditional methods from France and Europe, and is now open for breakfast, lunch and early dinners. From wonderful sandwiches on homemade breads to delicate crepes and cream pasta dishes, you'll love every single item on the menu. Just save room for an unforgettable dessert! Visit www.themainbakery.com or call 817-424-4333.

Customers often ask Dan Weinberger if his deli is a true Chicago eatery, and the answer is a resounding, "Yes!" Weinberger's Deli, 601 S. Main St., really is a perfect Chicago-style deli right in the heart of Grapevine's historic downtown. Dan was born on the south side of Chicago, and grew up in his father's deli, learning the business as he says, "at his father's apron strings." As an adult he trained to be a chef and went on to become a culinary consultant. He is now considered the "Sultan of Sandwiches," and with one visit, you're sure to know why." Weinberger's Deli is a sandwich emporium unlike any other, boasting almost 500 different flavor combinations. Dan carries Kelly Eisenberg and Vienna products from Chicago, and uses freshly baked breads for all of the sandwiches. Dan guarantees that if you don't absolutely love your sandwich he'll build you another one you will! "This is true comfort food," he says. Visit www.weinbergersdeli.com or call 817-416-5577.

Carolyn and Mark Rollins sum up their café this way: "Real good home-style cookin' brought to ya by some real friendly folk." Everyone at the OldWest Café, 600 W. Northwest Hwy. in Grapevine, is committed to making your breakfast or lunch an unforgettable experience, one you'll go back for again and again. Carolyn remembers the day Mark came home and handed her the keys to her very own café! Until then, she had been working for a major corporation and seeming never to have time for the important things in life, namely family and friends. That changed in 1997, with the opening of the first OldWest Café. Since then, the Rollins, along with their son Bill, have strived to create a place where you can enjoy delicious home-style meals with family and friends at all the locations. The OldWest Café's staff does its best to give great personal attention and premier service. Visit www.oldwestcafe.us or call 817-442-9378.

After 12 years in the hustle and bustle of the corporate accounting world, Patricia Wilson (Chef Patty) decided to follow her dream and passion of becoming a chef. With the support of her husband (who loves her cooking), she began working in several kitchens and bakeries before attending the Culinary School in Dallas. "I spent my nights as an overnight baker for Panera Bread and my days in school," she says. That training paid off with a job in the pastry kitchen of The Ritz-Carlton and eventually with her own Patty Cakes Bakery, 417 S. Main St. in Grapevine. She admits that nothing makes her happier than seeing the smiles on her customers' faces after eating her sweets. Everything is made from scratch, many of

the recipes have been passed down from her mother and grandmother. Two favorites? The Red Velvet Cupcakes and Chocolate Cakeballs. Chef Patty also offers cooking and decorating classes. Call 817-223-1471 or visit www.chefpattycakes.com.

Ask any local in Grapevine about the great seafood in town and they'll more than likely point you in the direction of Big Fish Seafood Grill and Bar, 414 S. Main St. It's a wonderful restaurant with a huge selection of fresh seafood, delicious sides and a few things thrown in the pot that don't actually swim for the non-fish lovers. From Big Fish tacos, huge po-boys and tasty crab cakes to baskets overflowing with crispy fried fish, fried shrimp or fried oysters, everything is delicious. With more than 20 years experience in the restaurant business, owner Michael Easley guarantees that everything is fresh and cooked to perfection. Wednesday nights are favorites, because that's when he turns on the boiling pot for an immense all-you-can-eat crawfish feast. There is live music on Wednesdays and Saturdays, but fun and absolutely yummy seafood every day of the week. Call 817-481-2010 or visit www.bigfishonmain.com.

Even as you walk up the manicured path to the stately three-story Queen Ann home you somehow know that your experience inside will be memorable. Sherry Jaquess has transformed the historic "Dorris House," 224 E. College St., into Renata Salon & Day Spa, one of the most respected salons in the state. Gleaming hardwood floors, Victorian antiques and elegant fireplaces inspire relaxation in a beautiful "home" setting. The rooms are decorated with plush furniture and beautiful stained glass windows. You'll be greeted with the laughter, smiles and genuine affection of the stylists, aestheticians and massage therapists. Offering the finest in skin care, hair and nail services, massage and body treatments, Renata has emerged as a top salon that has garnered accolades from across the country. It was featured on the TV show, *Split Ends*. *Sophisticates Hair Style Guide* named it "#1 Salon in the state of Texas," and *Color and Style* magazine listed it as one of the "Top 30 Hottest Salons Across the U.S."

Renata is indeed a special place of love. It's a place where women come for sweet conversation or encouraging words, a charming, fun place where they are accepted and loved—wet hair and all. An example of this heartfelt outreach to the community of Grapevine is Sherry's invitation to any woman going through chemotherapy. "When they are ready to shave their head, we invite them and their support group to cross this emotional landmark in complete privacy," she says, "It is a very vulnerable time, and we've never gotten through one of these ceremonies with dry eyes."

Visit www.renatasalons.com or call 817-488-3444. Be sure to ask about accommodations on the 3rd floor for parties.

Wines

Holly Donnelly stopped by Off the Vine one afternoon for a bottle of wine and commented to the previous owner on a few of the wine labels she recognized. "I was hired on the spot!" she says. Holly fell in love with the wine business, and now, as the new owner, offers customers incredible personal service and excellent choices of great wine. Located in one of Grapevine's lovely, historical buildings from the 1800s, Off the Vine, 324 S. Main St., is a wine boutique known for its unique wine selections and knowledgeable staff. "We usually carry about 300 labels—a case at a time," Holly says, "and when you visit the store you'll see staff tasting notes attached to each label." The customers become friends, and love the impromptu tastings with visiting winemakers, BYOB dinners and wine-paring dinners with local restaurants. Be sure to ask about the fabulous wine-themed gift baskets and locally made wine accessories. Visit www.offthevinetexas.com or call 817-421-1091.

Discover Weatherford

It's known as the Peach Capital of Texas and the Cutting Horse Capital of the World, and we think it's one of the most charming small towns in the Lone Star State. Weatherford has a rich Western heritage filled with interesting, colorful characters and is a perfect choice for a wonderful *Lady's Day Out* adventure. Just a few minutes west of Fort Worth and the Metroplex, it is a forward-thinking town that embraces growth and progress while honoring its unique history.

Visitors love the charm of the historical downtown with its beautiful original architecture, the excellent shopping opportunities, the famous **"First Monday Trade Days,"** a superb **Farmers Market**, and breathtaking, world-class gardens. You will love exploring all that Weatherford has to offer and learning about its rich tapestry of cattle barons, cowboys and Broadway stars. Weatherford was home to several characters that inspired the famous novel and mini-series *Lonesome Dove* by Larry McMurtry. It was based on the story of Oliver Loving's dying wish to his friend Charles Goodnight to be carried back to his homeland for burial. (You'll remember them as Rangers Call and McCrae in the book and movie.) Oliver is buried in Greenwood Cemetery, along with Boze Ikard for whom the character Deets was modeled. In fact, his headstone reads almost exactly as the one carved by Captain Call in the book:

"Served with me four years on the Goodnight-Loving Trail, never shirked a duty or disobeyed an order, rode with me in many stampedes, participated in three engagements with Comanches, splendid behavior. C. Goodnight."

Several other famous figures called Weatherford home, including the internationally known Broadway star Mary Martin, who we all knew and loved as Peter Pan, and her son Larry Hagman, (the infamous J.R. Ewing from the television melodrama *Dallas.*) Famed portrait artist Douglas Chandor moved to Weatherford when he married Ina Kuteman, and designed and built the incredible Chandor Gardens, which you'll read about in our book.

A Rich Western Heritage

Established in 1858, Weatherford was named for Senator Jefferson Weatherford, who sponsored the county and town's creation. Senator Weatherford, along with Representative Isaac Parker, created the petition for a 30-square-mile county to be carved from the territory west of Tarrant County. Two hundred twenty-four men signed the request that was carried by horseback to the capital in Austin, where the county was named for Representative Parker. The beautiful, ornate Parker County Courthouse stands today as the center of life in downtown Weatherford, and it has quite a history. It is, in fact, the fourth courthouse to have been built on the site. The first was a one-room, rough pine structure built in 1856 from lumber hauled from 300 miles away. Just two years later, in 1858, a second courthouse was built, and a jail added a short time after that. Fire destroyed the buildings in 1874, and a third courthouse was constructed in 1879. Incredibly, in 1884, the third courthouse was lost to fire as well, and the present structure was completed in 1886, with the ornate clock tower installed the following year. Recently renovated and open to the public, the beautiful Parker County Courthouse has one of the four largest courtrooms in all of Texas, with 4,500-square-feet of space and 28-foot ceilings.

The historic downtown shopping district surrounds the majestic courthouse, and the streets are lined with beautiful, historic buildings and homes, many renovated and restored to their original splendor.

You will also be able to learn about the town's rich history through the exhibits at the **Doss Heritage and Cultural Center of Parker County**. Established by James and Dorothy Doss, the Center takes visitors into the past—to the legendary trail drive named for Charles Goodnight; to the days when the Butterfield Stagecoach Line (which evolved into what we now know as the American Express Company and Wells Fargo) stopped in Weatherford, and into the everyday lives of the town's sturdy pioneers.

Weatherford's Chamber of Commerce is your first stop for excellent information. It is located in the historical Santa Fe Depot, which was built in 1908. The last train left the station platform in 1959, and the depot was designated a historic landmark in 1960.

The Extraordinary "Gardens" of Weatherford

There are two incredibly beautiful gardens in Weatherford that you absolutely must visit. The first is the world-class **Chandor Gardens**, created almost 70 years ago by the world famous English painter, Douglas Chandor. He and his wife Ina took a rock-filled caliche hill that included her mother's cow pasture, and began with picks, shovels and dynamite to create structured "garden rooms," filled with fountains, grottos and waterfalls. When Douglas died in 1953, Ina opened the magnificent gardens to the public, and the city of Weatherford purchased them in 2002. The Chandor grounds and mansion are now popular venues for weddings and special events.

Clark Gardens Botanical Park is another Weatherford treasure and is said to "awaken senses to the natural wonders of Texas." This garden is the love story of Max and Billie Clark, written, not in words, but created in the acres and acres of irises, roses and lilies. There is a Historic Tree Trail that contains more than 75 different historical trees that tell the story of famous people or places in American history. Each is the genuine offspring of trees that witnessed lives and events that shaped our history.

"Peachy Celebrations" and More

Weatherford says they grow the "biggest, sweetest, juiciest peaches in the state!" The State Legislature must agree, because Weatherford and Parker County has indeed been named "Peach Capital of Texas," and they sure know how to celebrate that honor.

Weatherford's largest one-day event, **The Peach Festival**, is held the second Saturday of July each year (the peak of the peach season) on the historic Weatherford Square. You'll be treated to peach pie, peach ice cream, peach crepes, peach— well, everything. It's a delicious day! More than 30,000 visitors gather each year to enjoy homemade arts and crafts, hometown entertainment and great food, and an abundance of the "biggest, sweetest, juiciest peaches" in Texas. There's even a baby diaper derby and a Peach Pedal bike ride.

A new event to the downtown is the **Weatherford Blooms Home and Garden Festival**. This one-day event takes place in late April and features arts and crafts, home and garden supplies, gardening seminars, and activities.

The town of Weatherford also celebrates its deep Western roots with fun events throughout the year. **The Cowboy Gathering** is a grand tribute to the town's famous cowboys. You will find chuck wagons and lots of Cowboy cuisine at this annual festival. The **Parker County Sheriff's Posse Rodeo** each June is one of the largest in Texas. Everyone in town shows up here with their cowboy boots on for the rodeo!

And, speaking of cowboys, and their horses, Weatherford boasts more cutting horses per capita than any other city, so you can watch some type of cutting horse event almost any weekend at the Silverado on the Brazos. The city hosts The Brazos Bash, (last week in September) one of the top-10 cutting events in the nation.

This small town lights up in a big way for the holidays with a **Candlelight Tour of Homes** in December, and shopkeepers around the square and throughout the town decorate their storefronts for the season. The sparkling lights and festive music make Weatherford an enchanting place to visit and shop. (We've got all the best tips for you!)

Outstanding Shopping

We love the history, the tributes, the festivals, the peaches, and in this town even the famous cemetery plots, but really, it's all about the *shopping!* You are in for such a treat as you meander through this small, Texas town because you are going to find wonderful, unique treasures at every turn. The historic buildings are now little antique shops, trendy boutiques, candle stores and great places to eat. You'll find Western furniture, fine collectibles, unique kitchen gadgets and great art. And if possible, plan to visit Weatherford for the **First Monday Trade Days,** held the weekend before the first Monday of each month. This wonderful tradition originated at the turn-of-the-century, when farmers and ranchers worked the land during the week and came into town on the weekend to buy, sell or trade their goods. Today the vendors are spread out over five acres at Santa Fe Drive and Fort Worth Highway. And, when you're through for the day, you'll find great places to rest up for your next day of fun in Weatherford!

For additional information on Weatherford, call 817-596-3801, 888-594-3801 or visit www.weatherford-chamber.com.

Weatherford Fairs Festivals & Fun

January
First Monday Trade Days

February
First Monday Trade Days
Sweethearts & Orphans Car
Show

March
First Monday Trade Days
Clark Gardens Spring Festival

April
First Monday Trade Days
Annual Spring Swing Golf
Tournament
Chandor Gardens Spring Fling
Books 'n Authors & All That
Jazz – Weatherford College
Weatherford Blooms

May
First Monday Trade Days
Greenwood Farm Horse Trials

June
First Monday Trade Days
Parker County Sheriff's Posse
Rodeo

July
First Monday Trade Days
Peach Festival / Peach Pedal

August
First Monday Trade Days
PBR Rodeo
Hot Dog Trot (5K & 1K)

September
First Monday Trade Days
Ranch Rodeo
Brazos Bash at Silverado
Cowboy Gathering
Greenwood Horse Trials

October
First Monday Trade Days
Talking Tombstone Tour
Chandor Gardens Goblins in
the Gardens
Clark Gardens Fall Festival
Miles 4 Mammograms (5K &
1K)

November
First Monday Trade Days
Coyote Chase (5K & 1K)

December
Christmas on the Square
Christmas Parade
Candlelight Tour of Homes

Main Street

MERCANTILE

The name itself lends a nostalgic tone to this wonderful antique store in Weatherford's historic downtown. Main Street Mercantile, 203 N. Main St., is located in one of the original old downtown buildings and, like all of them, has housed many businesses through the years. Today, it is filled with beautiful vintage lamps, fine antique furniture, vintage and new fabrics, Western artifacts, American Indian jewelry and books autographed by local authors. Owners Diana and Nick Hays have always loved antiques and have worked in the antique business for many years. Long-time residents of Weatherford and Parker County, they feel blessed to do something they love in such a wonderful town. "Our customers always feel welcome," says Diana. "They love the interesting way our merchandise is displayed, and always find something they can't leave without!" Browse this remarkable store, then pull up a seat for a cup of Arbuckle coffee or a real Sarsaparilla! Call 817-594-9670.

A STEP BACK'N TIME

As a young couple, Jim and Lori Perz became fascinated with vintage and antique furniture. They loved furnishing their home from garage and estate sales, as well as auctions. When there was no more room in their home, they began selling their unique finds out of their basement and eventually in 1999, they leased a building in Traverse City, Mich. When they moved to Weatherford in 2006, they once again began to buy more antiques than they could use and soon decided to open a store. A Step Back'n Time has allowed them the chance to get acquainted with their neighbors while continuing to buy antiques from around the world. They specialize in armoires and buffets—many pieces shipped from Liverpool, England.

"We love the relaxed, laid back atmosphere here in Weatherford," Lori says, "We love sharing our stories about the North and hearing all about our new Texas home!" One visit to 210 York Ave and we're sure you'll be enchanted by Jim and Lori. Call 817-594-5929 or visit www.stepbackntime.com.

Artists & Art Galleries

Weatherford Art Association
in the Firehouse Gallery & Art Center

The city of Weatherford is extremely fortunate to have an association of talented artists whose purpose is to promote the growth and appreciation of art in the community. The Weatherford Art Association was formed in 1977 and today is located in the historically designated Firehouse Gallery, 119 W. Palo Pinto St. The old firehouse still has the circular stairs and oversized garage doors but is now home to exhibits of original art and handmade pottery. Artists rent the studio spaces located within the gallery, and you'll often find them meeting and painting together. The WAA hosts six art shows and multiple workshops throughout the year. It is a great place to find incredible original art at reasonable prices and observe Artisans at work. For information on scheduled exhibits, call 817-599-3278 or visit www.weatherfordart.com.

CHANDOR GARDENS

When famed English portrait artist Douglas Chandor married Ina Kuteman in 1935, she convinced him to build their home and garden in the heart of her hometown of Weatherford. Together, they carved the world-class gardens from four acres of rough, rock-hard terrain with picks, shovels and dynamite. Mr. Chandor drew upon his experience as an artist to design the gardens with stunning views, waterfalls, intricate stonework and unique sculptures. Together, they created a paradise of beautiful garden rooms connected by meandering walkways.

When her husband died in 1953, Mrs. Chandor kept the gardens open to the public, but after her death in the 1970s, the property was left unattended and neglected for 20 years. Charles and Melody Bradford purchased Chandor Gardens in 1994 and painstakingly restored the overgrown gardens and home, returning it to all its former glory. The City of Weatherford bought the property at 711 W. Lee Ave. in 2002, and the gardens are once again open for tours. It is an incredible place of beauty—ideal for weddings, retreats, private parties and special events. Visit www.chandorgardens.com or call 817-613-1700.

Clark Gardens
BOTANICAL PARK

 Once a rugged mesquite pasture, the incredible Clark Gardens Botanical Park in Weatherford is now a botanical masterpiece showcased on 35 acres that entices visitors worldwide. It is a magical place where you can sense the love that inspired its beauty. Max Clark, born in 1927, began developing the gardens in 1972. Along the way, his wife Billie wanted to add an English-style Channel Garden for an upcoming iris show after seeing one in England. As Max recalls, "One thing led to another," and now with 50 gardens, evidently whatever Billie wanted—Billie got. Today, you can still see Max in the gardens working on his next creation. Their daughter Carol Clark Montgomery manages the nonprofit organization, which allows visitors to stroll trails of irises, tulips, lilies and roses. They can delight in waterfalls that cascade into ponds filled with swans and migrating ducks all while enjoying the wonders of nature "Texas style."

The grounds are a breathtaking kaleidoscope of color with more than 1,400 irises and thousands of cannas, daylilies, poppies and Crape Myrtles. Be sure to visit the Historical Tree Trail. It contains more than 100 trees that are direct descendents of trees that witnessed historically significant events in America. G-Scale model trains meander on 1200 feet of landscaped track, which replicate the areas historic rail system and towns.

Clark Gardens hosts four seasonal festivals annually and is a premier venue for weddings and special celebrations. Tiered walkways, majestic fountains and rose-covered arbors enhance the setting of the lighted pavilions, stately tented areas and lakeside gazebos that are picture perfect settings for both intimate and large parties.

Visit Clark Gardens at 567 Maddux Rd. and enjoy a true labor of love that took the Clarks over three decades to create. Or plan to stay just a short walk from the gardens in The Retreat, a beautiful secluded bed and breakfast with intimate interiors, trellised decks and open courtyards. For more information, call 940-682-4856 or visit www.clarkgardens.com. (*Color photo featured in front section of book.*)

Doss Heritage and Culture Center

Parker County is well known for its rich history and cultural contributions from cattle barons to cowboys, musicians to artisans, and Broadway stars to political leaders. The Doss Heritage and Culture Center opened in 2006 with the mission of preserving the county's important history. Civic Development, Inc. and the people of Parker County raised $6 million to house the center, with an initial gift of $1 million from Mr. and Mrs. James Doss, one of the area's pioneer ranching and banking families. The fabulous 23,000-square-foot facility at 1400 Texas Dr. in Weatherford sits on more than seven acres of pristine woods. The Doss Center is made up of three galleries, two of which hold an amazing collection of historical archives, artifacts, and memorabilia, which tell the history of Parker County and its citizens. In the third, one can enjoy national exhibits that periodically travel throughout the country.

The Heritage Gallery houses a permanent, interactive display that teaches about the beginnings of Parker County and pioneer life on the frontier. In the center of the lobby, you'll see a stagecoach, which has been preserved and reconstructed by J.W. Brown, and an authentic chuckwagon reminiscent of life on the cattle trail with Oliver Loving, the father of the trail driving period and his revered partner Charlie Goodnight. A second gallery is devoted to the famous actress Mary Martin (*Peter Pan*), who was born in Weatherford and her son Larry Hagman (known to most of us as J.R. Ewing in the series *Dallas.*)

The Doss Center also sponsors musical theater, summertime camps, Indian Studies week, chuck wagon cooking classes, gardening lessons and fabulous festivals. And, they are very proud of the ongoing educational programs that allow visitors to step back in history and experience the values and ethics of the pioneers who helped tame the Old West and settle Parker County. For more information, call 817-599-6168 or visit online at www.dosscenter.org. *(Color photo featured in front section of book.)*

Bed and Breakfasts & Cottages

When Gary and Lee Ann Gillespie stepped into the cozy bungalow at 212 E. Lee Ave., they knew at once they had found the perfect home for their bed and breakfast. Gary and Lee Ann have taken ideas from the many bed and breakfasts they've visited through the years and created a warm, inviting place of solitude close to Weatherford's historic square. The Rose Garden Cottage has two bedrooms and baths and a complete kitchen with coffee, tea and beverages included and can sleep up to five people. Lee Ann says, "We want our guests to feel as though they are in a private home, and we treat them the way we want to be treated." They have furnished The Rose Garden Cottage with beautiful antiques and luxurious linens, so the home is a place of quiet solace and comfort. The beautiful fenced backyard is surrounded by majestic trees, flower gardens, arbor, fountain and pond. Visit www.rosegardencottage.com or call 817-219-3435.

Angel's Nest

BED AND BREAKFAST

Sitting on the highest point in Parker County, and only one mile from the courthouse, the magnificent Angel's Nest Bed and Breakfast, 1105 Palo Pinto St., offers incredible views, luxurious guest rooms and "heavenly" amenities. This Weatherford landmark (c.1896) is a three-story Victorian home with four fireplaces, 10 rooms and balconies that are perfect for moonlit moments. Owner Candice Dyer has created an atmosphere of unparalleled luxury and romance in each room with special touches like flat panel televisions, comfy bathrobes, and sumptuous bedding—some rooms boast temperpedic mattresses, that make guests feel truly pampered. Jacuzzi tubs for two are in five of the rooms, and in two of the rooms, you'll find Jacuzzi hot-tub whirlpool spas that accommodate six on private porches along with TV, futon and glass-top table. A delicious breakfast is delivered to your bedroom door daily. Candice has truly created an "angel's nest," a romantic haven unmatched for its luxury and comfort. Visit www.angels-nest.com or call 817-599-9600. *(Color photo featured in front section of book.)*

Fashion & Accessories

RENDY
RULY boutique

"The way you dress and present yourself can affect your mood and how you feel about yourself," says Terri Hurlbert and Wendy Kelley. That belief spurred these two Weatherford natives to open Truly Trendy, a hometown boutique, where they could share their love of fashion and style with others. They have filled their boutique, 801 I-20 W, with bright, fun fashions and accessories that will make anyone feel confident about their personal style. One visit and you'll understand why the boutique was voted 2009 Best Women's Fashion in the *Weatherford Telegram* poll. You will find everything from loungewear and casual to classic evening fashions, and custom-designed jewelry to complete each look. And, don't miss the popular line of "Butterfly Shoes" in bright patterns and prints, ergonomically designed to strike that perfect balance of playful, comfortable and functional. Visit www.thebutterflyshoe.com or call 817-594-6873.

Sherry O. Watters now has customers from around the country (including several well-known celebrities like Larry Hagman) who request her one-of-a-kind creations. Something Special, 126 B York Ave. in Weatherford, is a thriving specialty store where you'll find unique jackets, skirts, vests, totes, and jewelry—all hand-painted and all with a little "something special." Sherry says that it all began in 1970 when she spilled something on a favorite blouse. She took out her acrylic paints and covered the stain with a beautiful design — that's how fabric paints were born. In 1987 Sherry opened her own business next door to her husband's office. The response was great and with the booming success, she courteously moved her husband upstairs and she took over all of the space downstairs! From short denim jackets and long Western dusters to casual tees and short sets, every item is a piece-of-art. So be sure to stop by and watch Sherry painting in her shop as she creates her next masterpiece. Call 817-599-0294 or visit www.sherryo.org.

Gifts & Interior Design and Décor

Rani Grandstaff is "sentimental" about a lot of things but especially when it comes to her sweet grandmother, Irene Duncan. Both Irene and Rani shared a love of home fragrances and candle making, and that love grew into a successful boutique. The duo began making candles back in 1998. Every candle is triple scented and comes in a variety of sizes with more than 40 fabulous fragrances. A few of our favorites were Tuscan Herb and French Market. You're sure to find a favorite! And, if you really love one in particular, she can make it as a reed diffuser, room spray or body lotion.

Along with the high-quality candles, Scentimentals, 211 York Ave. in Weatherford, is filled with remarkable fashion and gift items. David Kahn Jeanswear, JWLA and Twisted Heart are popular fashion favorites. Shannon Koszyk Jewelry, Lady Primrose and Poo-pouri are popular gift items. You can even pick up a pair of Crocs or pull on a pair of Old Gringo Boots.

Sadly, Irene passed away in late 2009, but Rani says, "Her spirit continues to glow." Rani keeps their dream alive as she continues to make delicious candles and hunt for unique fashion and gift ideas. Visit www.scentimentalsboutique.com or call 817-599-6066.

As you might guess by the name of her store, Darlene Green's favorite time of the year is fall. "I hate the extreme heat of summer," she says, "so when fall and 'pumpkin' season comes, I'm in my element." She's always been drawn to things made from copper, so she combined the two in naming her delightful store. The Copper Pumpkin, 1713 Bethel Rd., has been a favorite with customers since 1989. It's easy to see why it has been voted "Best Gift Shop in Weatherford" for three years in a row.

Of course, Darlene's success has been built over the last 40 years. When she first moved to the area in 1970, she began a small ceramics business out of her home. Her reputation and products developed a following throughout Texas. With the opening of The Copper Pumpkin, Darlene continued to give customers the best possible service and 2,400-square-feet of gifts, gourmet foods and collectibles. Darlene stands ready to make customers feel right at home with a smile, a hot cup of coffee and a variety of products for everyone's taste and age.

Darlene has a talent for decorating and uses antique or unusual items to display her treasures. Two Art Deco manikins hold Mary Francis handbags, and the doors to the cabinets are hand-painted flower seed packets. You'll love her selection of bath and body products from Niven Morgan and Archipelago Botanicals; the wonderful candles by Trapp and Aspen Bay; and the fabulous section of cookware and gourmet foods.

Holidays are always special at The Copper Pumpkin. During these festive months, the store is decorated top-to-bottom with seasonal treasures. Look for the beautifully painted mural on the building's front, and enjoy shopping one of Texas' most beloved gift boutiques. Call 817-598-0660.

Heritage House

Unique Gifts & Home Accessories

When Mary Lou Baumann's friends saw the 100-year-old building on York Street that she intended to "fix up" as a gift shop she says their first thoughts were, "It will be fun to see if you can pull this off!" They should have known better than to doubt the perseverance and abilities of this dynamite business owner once she makes up her mind. The Heritage House, 122 York Ave. opened in 2001, and is now a favorite place to find unique gifts and extraordinary treasures for the home.

Mary Lou attended college in New York City and spent many years as a business consultant for top-international companies. She says, "My expertise was in streamlining businesses (maintaining production with fewer personnel) so I was always the one who had to do the dirty work. In fact, I earned the title as The Terminator." It's not hard to see that this lifestyle can be wearing on anyone, and she eventually decided it was time to stay off planes and slow down. She found Weatherford and opened the Heritage House, where her abilities as a smart businesswoman, coupled with her keen eye for quality has resulted in one of the city's most loved places to shop.

As you browse through the remarkable rooms of the store you are sure to find something you can't leave behind—a beautiful piece of Italian pottery or handcrafted Arthur Court tray; a magnificent painting or handsome mirror; a gorgeous pillow, an incredible piece of designer jewelry and popular bath and body products. Mary Lou loves helping others find special items that will make their homes look and feel elegant and unique. Oh, and be sure to look for her adorable canine store greeter, Daisy. Call 817-341-1410.

Glenda Bullard has always loved decorating. Because she was constantly changing the paint colors of their home, moving things around and collecting antiques, her family convinced her to place some of her items in the family veterinary supply business. That tiny corner quickly overflowed into the warehouse next door, and then into her successful business, Back to Yesterday. The building at 112 E. Church St. on the historic square in Weatherford has an intriguing "yesterday" itself—it was once a Livery Repair for wagons and carriages. Then in 1966, Glenda's family purchased it for their business. It is now a collection of unique home décor and gifts that is constantly evolving. Customers love the "Old House" located within the store that was built with materials from the Old Church Parsonage from Glenda's hometown. You'll also find a full line of Lampe Berger lamps and oils and fabulous jewelry and purses by Treska. There are treasures for all ages! Call 817-594-4777.

Whether you are looking for a unique painted armoire, a wrought iron mirror, a zebra rug or even an authentic Texas Longhorn for your wall, you'll find it all (and so much more) at two truly unique Weatherford stores. Owners Ron and Tammy McBee have filled Western Heritage Furniture & Accessories (1525 Fort Worth Hwy.) and The Design Center (1535 Fort Worth Hwy.) with distinctive furniture and accessories that will transform any home or ranch. Throughout both stores, you'll find handsome rugs, beautiful leather sofas and rustic tables, luxurious bedding and bath décor, Tyler Candles, and beautiful items that provide an unusual ambiance to any space. They have an unmatched selection of furniture that can be customized to fit any style or personality, and offer professional design services to help make any room shine. Visit www.westernheritageweatherford.com or call 817-594-1581.

Hotels & Inns

You will have all of the amenities of a first-class La Quinta, but experience the warmth of small-town America. Raj Patel was the first La Quinta franchise owner in Texas and expanded his business to Weatherford in 2002. He found the town to be one of the most welcoming, friendly places he had ever known. "We wanted to become one of the best in our industry in our location," he says. "What we learned was that to become the best you have to be 'loved' by the best." He loves the genuine feeling of community in Weatherford and strives to extend that warmth to each guest. The Inn is modern, featuring a sundeck around the heated outdoor pool and Jacuzzi, top-notch workout rooms and meeting facilities for up to 100 guests. La Quinta Inn and Suites, 1915 Wall St., is an excellent home base while exploring historic Weatherford or enjoying the big city sports and entertainment venues of Dallas and Fort Worth. The Texas-friendly staff will make you feel right at home! Visit www.lq.com or call 817-594-4481.

Weatherford Lodgings

America's Best Value Inn
817-599-3800
1110 Fort Worth Hwy.
www.americasbestvalueInn.com

Angel's Nest Bed & Breakfast
(See related story page 89.
Also color photo featured in front section
of book.)
817-599-9600
1105 Palo Pinto St.
www.angels-nest.com

Best Western
817-594-7401
1927 Santa Fe Dr.
www.bestwesterntexas.com

Candlewood Suites
215 Alford Dr.
817-599-9112
877-226-3539
www.candlewoodsuties.com

Comfort Inn & Suites
817-599-3300
210 Alford Dr.
www.comfortsuites.com

Econo Lodge
817-599-3705
1-866-599-3705
2207 Old Dennis Rd.
www.econolodge.com

Express Inn & Suites
817-599-3700
2500 S. Main St.
www.xpressinn.com

Fairfield Inn & Suites
817-599-4040
175 Alford Dr.
www.marriott.com

Hampton Inn
817-599-4800
2524 S. Main St.
www.hamptoninn1.hilton.com

Holiday Inn Express
Hotels & Suites
817-341-6299
850 E. I-20
www.ichotelsgroup.com

La Quinta Inn & Suites
(See related story page 96.)
817-594-4481
1915 Wall St.
www.LQ.com

Mama's Wish Bed & Breakfast
817-477-4184
414 W. Lee Ave.
www.mamas-wish.com

Motel 6
817-594-1740
150 Alford Dr.
www.motel6.com

Quality One Motel
817-594-0055
2213 Old Dennis Rd.

Quest Inn
817-594-3816
1106 W. Park Ave.

Rose Garden Cottage Bed & Breakfast
(See related story page 88.)
817-219-3435
212 E. Lee Ave.
www.rosegardencottage.com

Sleep & Go
817-599-0500
1709 E. I-20
www.sleepgo.net

Sleep Inn
817-594-9699
1911 Wall St.
www.sleepinn.com

Super 8 Motel
817-598-0852
720 Adams Dr.
www.super8.com

Super Value Inn
817-594-8702
866-539-0036
111 W. I-20

Victorian House Retreat
817-475-9009
110 E. 5th St.
www.victorianhouseretreat.com

Western Motel
817-599-8683
809 Palo Pinto St.

A parking lot full of cars and trucks is always a good sign that the food you're about to eat is great! The Mesquite Pit, 1201 Fort Worth Hwy. in Weatherford, continues to satisfy regulars and visitors from across Texas with delicious pit-smoked barbecue and homemade specialties. Try the thick, grilled rib eye, smoked prime rib, pork ribs or baked potato stuffed with chopped barbecue. Wes and Robin Maynard both grew up in Parker County, are the nicest people you'll meet, and pretty good cooks too! Robin's homemade desserts include warm bread pudding, old-fashioned buttermilk pie and banana pudding. They have created a warm, rustic, family atmosphere with lots of antiques, and have even added an 1880s bar—salvaged from the downtown square. Mesquite Pit serves up great Texas barbecue and genuine Southern hospitality. Be sure and visit the second location (owned by their son Jacob) in Mineral Wells at 3915 Mineral Wells Hwy. Visit www.mesquitepit.com or call 817-596-7046.

WEATHERFORD DOWNTOWN Cafe

It's a down-home café with an informal atmosphere, one of those wonderful small town places that are crowded with locals enjoying the great food and friendly banter. The Weatherford Downtown Café, 101 Church St. has been described as "old-school flavor with new South influence," and the results are delicious! Owner Britton Schweitzer (who graduated from Weatherford High School in 1989) has been in the restaurant business since the 1980s and earned his management stripes at Michaels and Daddy Jack's in Fort Worth. He even fashioned a movie/grill concept in Fort Worth before moving back to Weatherford with his wife Jamie and opened first the Fire Oak Grill and then Weatherford Downtown Café. Britton has turned over the reigns to the Fire Oak Grill and is now concentrating only on the Café with the sell of the Grill.

Originally a pharmacy, the one-story brick building features a large mural promoting the Parker County Peach Festival—held annually the second Saturday of July—original artwork on the walls, an open kitchen, a blackboard sporting the daily specials and a menu full of classic country dishes.

Breakfast choices include fluffy pancakes and syrup, French toast, eggs and country ham, omelets and spicy Tex-Mex. The lunch plates are huge—everything from classic chicken fried steak and mashed potatoes with cream gravy to fajita quesadillas and blackened Tilapia. Homemade bread and mouth-watering desserts are a great finish to a delicious meal, and everything is served-up with great big smiles and friendly, small-town hospitality. In fact, the Weatherford Downtown Café is the epitome of an old-fashioned Café and gathering place. Some folks come so often that the waitresses have their order ready when they get there! Oh yes, be sure to ask about the Café's supposedly spooky (but friendly) ghost! For more information, visit www.weatherforddowntowncafe.com or call 817-594-8717.

The sign on the building that accompanies Yesterdays Sandwich Shop's name is "homemade bread." And it's that very homemade bread that keeps the folks coming back. Yesterdays, 128 York Ave. in Weatherford, is owned by Debbie and Jeff Hicks, a delightful couple who has built quite a reputation for great sandwiches, delicious soups, snap-fresh salads, and scrumptious desserts. Their signature item—wonderful white or wheat sourdough bread—is baked fresh daily, sold in loaves and used for all of the sandwiches. Debbie says, "Our most requested sandwich is the homemade chicken salad on our homemade bread, and customers love the blackberry, peach and pecan cobblers." Jeff retired from his career as a full-time electrician to run their second location at 6239 FM 920, but he's still a volunteer firefighter. They also deliver to businesses for lunch meetings, and offer catering services for parties. Call 817-599-3903.

Salons, Spas & Indulgence

Long-time salon employees Debbie Arwood and Debra McCullough became partners in 1994, when they took a chance and opened Debonair Salon Spa in Weatherford. Debra comes from a long line of salon owners and remembers playing in her grandmother's salon as a child. Now her daughter works with her, and her granddaughter comes in to visit and play. With their exceptional expertise and sincere love for people, Debbie and Debra have built special relationships with their clientele that have stood the test of time. And, as members of the beauty industry, they have stepped up to the next level by treating the whole person in a relaxing and warm environment. Their packages include massage, facials, body masques, herbal steam saunas and hair, skin and nail care. They carry wonderful products from TIGI, as well as home décor items. Even the artwork on the walls from local artisans can be purchased! Stop by 520 Santa Fe Dr., visit www.debonairsalon.com, call 817-599-4071 or 817-341-7542.

East Texas

Carthage

Henderson

Kilgore

Mineola

Discover Carthage

The town of Carthage likes to brag that they are, "The Best Small Town in Texas!" Stroll the picturesque downtown sidewalks; revisit history at the Panola County Heritage Museum and Old Jail; see the exciting Texas Country Music Hall of Fame and meet the friendly business owners and locals. We think you'll agree that it just might be!

Carthage Recognition

Carthage was recognized in 2010 as one of 56 National Main Street Cities in Texas, and the honor was well deserved. The business owners have followed their leaders in rebuilding, renovating and growing their businesses, while holding to the rich heritage and history of Panola County.

The town was named in honor of Carthage, Mississippi, and the first post office and courthouse were built in 1849. The courthouse, made of peeled pine logs was used until 1853, when a new brick structure was built. The second courthouse was used until a third was built in 1885. In 1891, the first permanent jail was erected—a red brick building with iron doors, bars and cells. It was used until 1953 when the county built a new courthouse and jail. You can tour the historic Panola County's **Old Jail Library** on North Shelby Street, which is listed on the national Register of Historic Places, and now houses the **Panola County Historical and Genealogical Association**. Interesting items include the Roster of Confederate Soldiers, pioneer store ledgers and Panola County family histories.

On the southwest corner of the downtown square, the restored Bank Building is now home to the Panola County Texas Tea Room & Heritage Museum. Inside you can step back in time on a self-guided tour of Panola County that includes period dress, videos, photographs and great exhibits. The Texas Tea Room is onsite and operated by the Heritage Guild and offers delicious lunches in a nostalgic atmosphere. It's a wonderful place to pause during your visit for a decadent slice of Almond Joy Cake or Texas Tea Sludge Pit Pie!

Hall of Fame!

Country music is always big in Texas, but it is celebrated in a huge way in Carthage. As home to the **Texas Country Music Hall of Fame**, this small town entertains in a big way, honoring some of the biggest country musical stars in the U.S. A life-size bronze statue of Panola County's famous son, Maurice "Tex" Ritter, and his horse, "White Flash," welcome visitors to the Hall of Fame. The museum honors country musicians, songwriters and disc jockey legends and showcases memorabilia of all of the Hall of Fame members. The Tex Ritter section includes items from his home, while the Jim Reeves section highlights the authentic radio station equipment that he used during his early broadcasts. Three miles east of Carthage on Highway 79 North, a 12-foot statue marks the burial site of Jim Reeves along with his faithful dog—Cheyenne. A special ceremony is held each August to honor the new inductees.

For additional information, call the Carthage Chamber of Commerce at 903-693-6634 or visit www.carthagetexas.com.

Carthage Fairs Festivals & Fun

January
Martin Luther King Parade
Annual Lions Show

April
Main Street Quilt Show

May
Panola Co. PRCA Rodeo, BBQ & Parade

June
Texas Country Music Hall of Fame Showcase Auditions

August
Annual Texas Country Music Hall of Fame Showcase &
Awards Show

October
East Texas Oil & Gas Blast
St. Williams Catholic Church Cajun Fest

November
"All that Glitters" Gala Auction & Taste of Carthage

December
Carthage Book Club Home Tour
Carthage Christmas Parade
Breakfast with Santa

Antiques

The Cottage

Sandy Griffin loves collecting antiques almost as much as she loves cooking, and the result is The Cottage Tea Room & Antiques, 609 N. St. Mary's St. in Carthage. "I opened the tea room as an outlet for my antiques," she says. "I love being able to offer my customers (and friends) a pretty place to enjoy a wonderful lunch and the opportunity to shop for the treasures I find!" Built in 1948, The Cottage is known as "The Bingham House." Sandy has decorated several dining rooms with beautiful antiques that are for sale. Recently, she was able to show off the changes she's made to The Cottage during a visit from the descendants of the house's original owners. It was a thrill Sandy will never forget! Her customers rave about her delicious Chicken Salad and decadent "Sludge Pitt Pie." She also offers a remarkable four-course Valentine dinner with a local chef that includes a romantic horse-drawn carriage ride. For more information, call 903-693-2282.

Attractions, Entertainment & Museum

PANOLA COUNTY HISTORICAL AND GENEALOGICAL ASSOCIATION & OLD JAIL LIBRARY

The historic Panola County Jail was built in 1891 at 213 N. Shelby St. in Carthage and was used until 1954. When the Panola County Historical and Genealogical Association (PCHGA) was founded in 1987, it obtained a lease on the old jailhouse, which by this time had fallen into a state of disrepair. Committed to preserving family and local history, the Association raised money and donated their own time and resources to restore and renovate the old jail. It now has a new life housing history, family books and artifacts, and is open to the public three days a week. The upstairs, with cellblock locks still intact, is a museum, and the bottom floor (where the jailer's family lived and meals were prepared for prisoners) now has three book rooms with a good representation of state, county, and family history, a computer room and the PCHGA. Volunteers are available to assist you with your genealogical research and tour groups are welcome. For information, visit www.oldjaillibrary.org or call 903-693-3388.

Children's Shops

Retirement was just a new beginning for Frances Hoell, who after many years as a Business Operation Manager for the local hospital embraced a totally new direction in her life. With the help of her daughter Tracy she opened Mulberry Bush, a fabulous children's clothing and gift boutique at 450 W. Panola St. in Carthage. "We feel God has truly blessed us with this opportunity," Frances says, "and we try to provide great customer service to our loyal customers. We treat them the way we want to be treated." From classic sweet to trendy and fun, Mulberry Bush offers incredible clothing for newborn through size 4T for boys and newborn through size 14 for girls. You'll find beautiful things from Peaches 'n Cream, Bailey Boys, Zootie Patootie, Baby Nay and Feltman Brothers, to name a few. There is also a baby registry and a large selection of gift items for all ages, including personalized napmats, blankets, backpacks and more. Call 903-693-3833.

Fashion & Accessories

Patricia Smith is known as the "Prom Diva" with the largest selection of prom and special event clothing in the ArkLaTex. She opened Beauty Sense by Patricia,104 E. Sabine St., in 1985, and it has since become the place to buy prom dresses, bridesmaids dresses, tuxedos and ladies' apparel, like City Girl, Windridge, Sharon Young and Joseph Ribkoff. The 10,000-square-foot historical building is located on the historic downtown square right next to the Texas Tea Room, and has such a large inventory it's hard to see it all. Patricia is all about "beauty" in every sense, from gorgeous prom and quinceañera dresses to beauty products such as Vitabath, Niven Morgan and even her own cosmetic line. Collectibles from Jim Shore, Lenox, Vera Wang, line the shelves. It's a wonderful store to browse for unique and fun gifts, and includes both a bridal and baby registry service. For more information, call 903-693-2871. This store you do not want to miss!

Gifts, Home Décor & Jewelry

The Hobby Horse is truly "A Carthage Tradition" that began in 1973. Like her predecessors, Owner Bonnie Pauler continues to offer a variety of irresistible gifts and home décor. The quaint and charming building that houses this scrumptious boutique was built in the 1930s and still retains its original floors and character. The Hobby Horse is located at 119 W. Sabine St. in Panola County's Historic District. You will find beautiful frames, baby items, jewelry, fashion accessories, candles and even ice cream! It is a favorite place for many brides with an extensive bridal registry, filled with prized selections of china and crystal. Marque name brands like Waterford, Arthur

Court, Vagabond House, and Juliska fill this shop, and its staff is always ready to help you make the perfect choice for your pocketbook. Don't miss The Hobby Horse; you will walk away saying, "I love that store!" Call 903-693-9327 for more information.

Copper Falls & Co.
Jewelry • Gifts • Accessories

This was a business that was destined to be. Owners Tommy Moore and Melinda Leslie have been friends and coworkers since 1989, but it took them years to finally partner in opening Copper Falls & Co. This remarkable full-service jewelry store specializes in custom design and in-house jewelry repair. Most Carthage locals will remember the historic building at 108 E. Sabine St. as Jenkins' Drugs, but it was originally built in 1916 as Hooker's Pharmacy. Today, the superb jewelry and gift store boasts the original 12-foot-tall pressed ceiling and handsome Cherry wood and glass built-in cabinets with the authentic roll up glass case doors. There are also three copper waterfalls in the store, which helped with the name selection!

Tommy and Melinda have a combination of more than 50 years of experience in the jewelry business. Tommy and his wife Debbie moved to Carthage from Louisiana in 1989 to buy Cox's Jewelry, and Melinda came to work for them that same year. She stayed with them for nine years as a bench jeweler, but left in 1999 to open a business with her husband Rickey. The two remained friends and continued to dream about co-owning a jewelry story. When they found this wonderful building in the Carthage main street square,

they knew it would be perfect for the store they had always envisioned.

You'll find everything from basic silver chains to to spectacular diamonds and gemstones. They also carry a large selection of estate and vintage jewelry, wonderful fashion jewelry by Treska and Mei Mei's Designs, and unique gift items from Crosses, Bridgewater Candles, Caren Original, NAPA patio firelites, and Killin N Grillin merchandise. It's a beautiful store! For more information, call 903-693-9944.

There aren't many pharmacies in the country that still offer old-fashioned customer service like free delivery and personal charge accounts. This dedication to personal care and service has been a trademark of Ken Turner Pharmacy from its very beginning, and that's just one of the things that their loyal customers appreciate. The original part of the store, 109 E. Panola St., was built in 1947 for Rand Drug. Ken purchased this Carthage business in 1961 and eventually added a building next to it to enlarge the space. He was working in Tyler, Texas, as a pharmacist, when he found this pharmacy for sale, and knew that it would be the perfect business for him and his family. Ken Turner Pharmacy is all about "family," by caring for their customers' prescription needs and promoting healthy living and wellness, and by providing the extra special services like home delivery.

The store is also a fun place to shop. If you're a John Wayne fan, (who isn't?) you'll love the huge "Duke" collection, with everything from posters and pictures to mugs and collectibles. There is an interesting gun collection, great displays of collectible cars and even hunting supplies. There are gifts for everyone, from unique jewelry and fashion accessories to frames, books and home décor. You can also find the very popular Circle E Candles here, as well as great special occasion cards.

Unlike large chains, Ken Turner Pharmacy is a real "hometown" pharmacy—a place where everyone knows your name and is glad to see you. The staff does a great job of affirming the town's reputation as one of the friendliest places in the country. Call 903-693-7106.

Restaurants

While searching for a new business, Debbie Moore was incredibly impressed with the quality of the product and proven success of Buck's Pizza. She knew it would be a big hit with the natives of Carthage. She was right! The food is delicious—from oven-baked hoagies and puffy Stromboli to more than 20 specialty, build-your-own pizzas. Not just a "pizza place" Buck's also serves fresh salads, pastas and even crispy, hand-breaded chicken tenders. There is something for everyone, and it's all delicious. The intangible treat at Buck's Pizza, 1020 W. Panola St., (in addition to the great food) is the outstanding customer service. The entire staff is very friendly and helpful, and you get the idea that you are the most important person in the room. From classic pepperoni and sausage to Hawaiian and barbecue chicken, every pizza is perfect! Visit www.buckspizza.com or call 903-690-0400.

Discover Henderson

"Discover" the excitement of upscale shopping in one of the prettiest downtown squares in East Texas; step back in time and onto one of the highest points in Rusk County while visiting Monte Verdi Cotton Plantation and the Howard-Dickinson House; get sticky and sweet at the Heritage Syrup Festival and relive some of the most exciting and most tragic moments in Henderson and Rusk County's history at local museums. Located in the heart of East Texas, this designated "Texas and National Main Street City" boasts a beautiful National Register Historic Downtown Square. Those impressive titles should be enough to make you want to visit this charming community, but just wait till you see what we've discovered in historic Henderson!!

Henderson History

Founded in 1843, Henderson is older than the state of Texas itself. One of the city's founding fathers, W.B. Ochiltree, gave 10 acres of his land to the town site with the condition that it be named in honor of his friend, James Pinckney Henderson. Henderson became the first governor of Texas, later served as the first Attorney General of the Republic of Texas and even later as Secretary of State.

The town of Henderson became the county seat of Rusk County, named after James P. Henderson's law partner, Thomas Jefferson Rusk, also important in early Texas history. At one time,

Rusk County had more than two dozen cotton plantations of 10,000 acres or more. Today, the town and the county have many historical markers that include historic homes, churches, schools and cemeteries. Tragedy struck in 1860 when 43 buildings on the town's square burned to the ground. An abolitionist plot was suspected, and when Texas withdrew from the Union, Rusk County sent more men to serve in the Civil War that any other part of Texas. Downtown buildings were rebuilt during the 1880s with architectural styles like Victorian Italianate, Romanesque Revival and Art Deco, and the square is now a National Register Historic District.

A planned Galveston, Houston and Henderson Railroad wasn't completed after the Civil War and Henderson's path to growth ended for a while. The town and the area relied on agriculture—especially the growing of cotton—until like its neighbor Kilgore, the discovery of black gold at the drilling site of Daisy Miller Bradford #3 in 1930 changed its fortune and future. Wildcatter C.M. "Dad" Joiner discovered oil just six miles from town, ushering in a huge oil boom that caused a population growth from 2,000 to more than 10,000 in just a few months. The establishment of a brick plant—Henderson Clay Products—also brought jobs, and the community managed to prosper through the decades despite up and down economic times. Today, Henderson continues to be one of the most charming and picturesque downtowns in the East Texas area. Take the Historic Downtown Walking Tour and enjoy the visual history of this beautiful town. One of the most elegant and historic houses in Henderson is the **Howard-Dickinson House**, which was built in 1855 by carpenter/brickmakers Dave and Logan Howard. It is now open for tours and special events. Located at 501 South Main St., this house is not-to-be-missed.

A Generation Lost

March 18, 1937 began as a typical day for London School near Henderson. Children took math tests, ran laps in the gym, gossiped in the cafeteria and packed their bags with homework. Little did the students and teachers know that a large crawl space that ran the entire 253-foot length of the building's facade held odorless and colorless gas that had been leaking from the gas line tap. It was estimated that there were almost 600 students and 40 teachers in the building, with a PTA meeting in session in an adjoining building.

Sometime between 3:05 and 3:20 PM, someone turned on an electric sander. It is believed that the sander's switch created a spark that ignited the trapped gas-air mixture, causing an explosion so great that a two-ton concrete block was thrown clear of the building, crushing a car parked nearby. Witnesses reported that the walls of the school bulged, the roof lifted from the building, then crashed back down, collapsing the main wing of the structure. More than 300 children, teachers and visitors were killed. The explosion was heard for miles, and within minutes parents and residents began to arrive, digging through the rubble with their own hands. Roughnecks from nearby oil fields rushed with equipment to help clear the concrete and steel and search for survivors. Help began to pour in from outside the community and state, and news people rolled into town for the story. Walter Cronkite covered the school explosion as one of his first assignments for the United Press, and was quoted decades later as saying, "I did nothing in my studies nor in my life to prepare for a story of the magnitude of that New London tragedy, nor has any story since that awful day equaled it." It has become known as "The Day A Generation Died."

As soon as the site was cleared and buildings were cleaned, classes resumed just 10 days later. A new school was completed in 1939, directly behind the location of the destroyed building and was renamed West Rusk High School. A large granite cenotaph across from the school commemorates the 1937 disaster, as does the **London Museum & Tea Room** just across the street, which chronicles and honors the many people who lost their lives that terrible day. All gas today is infused with an odor because of this tragedy.

Henderson Museums

One of our favorite things to do as we travel is to get acquainted with the history of the town or city we are discovering. The best places to start are the museums. Henderson's museums chronicle the history, excitement, pride, sorrow and hope of East Texas, and provide families with days of entertainment.

The **Depot Museum** complex houses the Rusk County History Museum and the Children's Discovery Center. Twelve restored buildings span five acres, showcasing the richness of Rusk County's history. Begin your visit at the Arnold building, where you'll see exhibits about Indians, settlers, schools and oil wildcatters. Another building contains a cotton gin restored from its former location in Mt. Enterprise. Get up close to the sawmill, which still operates during the annual Heritage Syrup Festival. The largest budding onsite is the restored 1901 Missouri-Pacific depot, which includes a hands-on Children's Discovery Center. Other structures on the grounds include a Doctor's Office, General Store, Print Shop, and a genuine settler's cabin, the T.J. Walling Log Cabin. Children will love the 1950s era carousel that still operates. Perhaps the most unusual exhibit at the museum is the Arnold Outhouse. According to author Bob Bowman, "This Victorian deluxe outhouse was awarded a Texas Historical Marker, giving Henderson legitimate claim to fame as the location of the Fanciest Little Outhouse in Texas"!

Drive just a few miles west of Henderson on Hwy. 64 to the **Gaston Museum** (along the Oil Field Driving Tour) and be transported back to life in a 1930s East Texas Oil Patch. The Gaston Museum at Joinerville, is Rusk County's newest museum in a 1940s roadside cafe building. Tour an oil field tent house and a Dixie Service Station that was established in 1931, and see exhibits about the early oil field boom, radios from the 1930s to the 1950s, and memorabilia from World War II, the Korean War and the Vietnam War.

Festivals and Fun

Spend time learning the history and heritage of Henderson, then park your car in the downtown square and begin your exciting discovery of everything there is to offer in this charming town. There are upscale clothing and gift boutiques, jewelry stores, antique shops and a variety of eateries that will satisfy and please. One thing that makes this downtown square such a delight to shop is that it is so "comfortable." Colorful canvas awnings decorate the historic buildings and offer shade to the shoppers (and gentlemen in waiting)! Everyone is friendly and helpful and as sweet as Henderson's famous cane syrup!

The tradition of ribbon cane syrup making is commemorated every year at the annual **Heritage Syrup Festival**, held the second Saturday of November on the Depot Museum grounds and downtown. Syrup makers operate the antique, mule-powered equipment to make old-fashioned cane syrup. There are also artists demonstrating techniques for basket weaving, rope making, woodcarving, quilting and lace making. Singers entertain, and there is a petting zoo for little ones. The Syrup Festival spreads from the Depot to Heritage Square, where you can continue to browse more than 250 booths with a variety of offerings, enjoy musical stage entertainment, clogging and square dancing, and even see a melodrama at the Opera House. If you haven't had just as much fun as you can possibly imagine, load the family onto the 4-H trailer for a hayride back to the Depot. Take home a bottle or jar of old-fashioned cane syrup as a memento of your "sweet" experience in Henderson's charming downtown.

Other special events held in Henderson are "An Affair of the Arts" art walk in the spring, "Birthday Party for America" in July, "Country Fair on the Square" in the fall and "Home for the Holidays in Henderson" first weekend in December. For more information, see www.visithendersontx.com or www.mainstreethenderson.com. *(Color photo featured in front section of the book.)*

For additional information, call the Henderson Area Chamber of Commerce at 903-657-5528 or Henderson Tourism at 866-650-5529.

GO TEXAN.

★CERTIFIED★

RETIREMENT COMMUNITY

Henderson Fairs Festivals & Fun

April

    East Texas Antique Tractor Show

May

    An Affair of the Arts Downtown Artwalk

July

    Birthday for America Patriotic Parade & Fireworks

August

    East Texas Sacred Harp Singing Convention

October

    Country Fair on the Square
    Rusk County PRCA Rodeo

November

    Heritage Syrup Festival

December

    Christmas Historic Home Tour Home for the Holidays

HENDERSON

AREA CHAMBER OF COMMERCE

Dedicated to shaping and promoting the future of the town and surrounding area, the Henderson Area Chamber of Commerce is comprised of a dedicated group of members who are committed to preserving the uniqueness of their community. Founded in 1926, the Chamber is presently located at 201 N. Main St. in a historic Sinclair service station that was remodeled in 1979. Be sure to visit the Web site—www.hendersontx. com— for information on many exciting events and opportunities in Henderson and throughout Rusk County. Learn about the Henderson Civic Theatre, spring and summer festivals—including the famous Heritage Syrup Festival in November—the Christmas parade and the Historic Downtown Walking Tour. The wonderful character of Henderson is continually being preserved and promoted, and the town has been designated a Texas Main Street Project City. Call 903-657-5528.

Antiques & Specialty Shops

The Curious Wren

Bill and Billie Brookshire feel very connected with the town they love. And how could they not—their business is right in the middle of historical downtown Henderson. The Curious Wren, 123 S. Main St., is a lovely store filled with beautiful collections of antiques, estate jewelry, dolls and the fabulous Thymes bath and body products. Bill and Billie have had a lot of fun collecting antiques and vintage jewelry through the years. Billie says that her mother inspired her fascination with antiques as a child. She's loved them ever since. Billie first opened The Doll House in 1990 with a popular selection of Madame Alexander Dolls and well-known collectibles. When that building sold, she and Bill decided to open The Curious Wren as an outlet for their passion of antiques and Bill's musical talents. He plays the guitar, the mandolin and the banjo and enjoys playing music with his friends! It's a wonderful store with wonderful people! Call 903-655-1234.

Kids love this store, because it's "where pigs fly!" Really. There are bright pink walls, a zebra ceiling and pigs on the roof! Kid Kraze, 606 E. Main St., is an exciting, bright and happy place to shop for children's fashions, accessories and fun.

Owner Tracie Bowman has turned the charming house off Henderson's downtown square into an incredible children's boutique with lots of bling. In fact, she says that is one of her specialties. "We will custom-bling anything—shirts, cheer shorts, dresses or backpacks." Kid Kraze is a wonderful selection of children's clothing from size 0-3 months to size five. It's a one-stop store for everything from diaper bags and onesies to tutus and hair bows. Tracie carries popular lines such as Mud Pie Baby and Peaches 'n Cream, and fun jewelry for kids (and moms) of all ages. She also supplies the school uniforms that no one else has and items for favorite sports teams and mascots.

There is always something fun and exciting going on at Kid Kraze. There are special items for happy "moms-to-be," great birthday gifts, lots of school spirit and many celebrations within the store. In fact, Tracie held the store's birthday party with hidden specials, balloons and birthday cake! She is an energetic and successful business woman with a true knack for marketing, display and great customer service. She knows which bows, headbands, flip flops and purses the kiddos love and makes it easy for moms to say "yes." There is a baby registry, and specials are always posted on Facebook. The store with the flying pigs is a favorite for all ages! Call 903-657-1465.

Cafés, Coffee & Restaurants

Claudia's Café & Catering
for any occasion, or no occasion at all

With its scrumptious breakfasts, delicious lunches and deca-dent desserts, Claudia Morgan-Gray and husband Weldon Gray have been making a name for themselves in Henderson since open-ing their delightful café and catering company in 2005. As owners of Claudia's Café & Catering, 202 US Hwy. 79 N., they were nomi-nated to compete in the "Ultimate Hometown Grill-Off Contest" on the *Live! with Regis and Kelly* TV show. Weldon's "Southern Smoked Pulled Pork with Sassy Sauce" was one of the finalists ... and their customers know why! Customers have voted Claudia's Café Henderson's Best Caterer, Best Cook and Best Deli. Enjoy a cup of freshly brewed coffee and a "not your mama's" oatmeal, a hot lunch special or specialty sandwich. Save room though, for something wonderful from the "Sweet Shop," like a slice of Dulce' de Leche Cheesecake. Everything is delicious and they even offer gourmet to go! Call 903-657-8420.

This quaint coffee café is much more than a great place to get a good cup of joe. It's an intimate place where friends can gather for breakfast, meet for lunch, enjoy live entertainment by locals and shop for wonderful art and gifts. Owners Amanda Harris and Travis Driver are proud that MoJoe's Coffee Café, 106 W. Main St., has become an integral part of the Henderson community. They have worked hard researching the business, remodeling the building and creating a comfortable coffee shop where families gather, and strangers become friends. It is also an outlet for Travis' art, as well as beautiful handcrafted gifts made by local artists. MoJoe's lunch menu offers a variety of Panini sandwiches, scrumptious soups, crisp salads and delicious homemade brownies! Call 903-392-8200 or stop by to get your MoJoe on!

TARBUTTON'S RESTAURANT & CATERING

Sandwiches, salads, burgers, steaks and "taters" like you've never tasted! For some of the most delicious cooking in the county, be sure you make the Tarbutton's Restaurant & Catering, 1307 US Hwy. 79 N. in Henderson, an absolute must! Michael and April Tarbutton invite you to be their guests, and taste what can only be described as "good ole home cookin." They have both been in the restaurant business since high school, and now combine their knowledge of the industry with their genuine, small town hospitality to make Tarbutton's a family favorite. From appetizers of bacon cheddar fries to juicy burgers, grilled Angus steaks and mouthwatering sides, everything is freshly prepared and delicious. Did we mention "taters?" Have you ever had Fried Chicken Taters, Taco Taters or even Barbecue Taters? Have those every day, but on Fridays order the crispy Fried Catfish with all the trimmings. Be sure to call ahead to see what dessert they have cooking in the kitchen today! Call 903-657-3474 or visit www.tarbuttons.com.

Fashion & Accessories

After an early retirement, Sam and Judy Hughes found a wonderful opportunity to get involved in their beloved hometown of Henderson and fulfill their dream of owning one of its Main Street businesses. With Judy's home economics and clothing construction and design knowledge, and Sam's background as a financial manager for Chevron, it was a natural move for them to buy B.J. Taylor & Co., an upscale boutique at 117 E. Main St. The historical building that houses this shop has had many lives through the years, but today it is filled with classic, contemporary clothing and accessories for those with a busy lifestyle. Shoppers will find everything from jeans to silk jackets and separates, as well as shoes and handbags. The jewelry line is handcrafted by two local artisans who love to fulfill custom-design orders. Sam and Judy are committed to outstanding customer service, and offer alterations and complimentary gift wrap. Call 903-657-9210. *(Color photo featured in front section of book.)*

Hearthstone Gallery

Find a trendy new outfit, buy an original piece of art, and get your hair done all at the same time! Hearthstone Gallery, 114 E. Main St., is a delightful store owned by mother-daughter team Mary Hall and Marci Davis. This duo bought the historic building in downtown Henderson in 2004 and have restored its original charm, with exposed-brick walls and beautiful oak floors. Mary showcases her original oil paintings and decorative furniture, while Marci is the fashion, accessory and gift buyer. Her unique flair is evident in the trendy styles throughout the store. Keeping it all in the family, Mary's son (and Marci's brother) Todd Davis designs one-of-a-kind jewelry that complements the contemporary fashions. There are also two hair stylists who rent space in the building. It's a great, fun store where, besides art and clothes, you'll find everything from delicious candles to wonderful soaps to Old World Christmas ornaments. Call 903-657-7057.

JORDAN'S PLANT FARM

Carol and James Jordan established this Henderson family-owned "plant farm" in 1976, with only one greenhouse and a lot of imagination. Today, it is not only one of the finest nurseries and garden centers in the state, but has become a huge East Texas tourist attraction. The 500,000 square feet of growing space, garden center and gift shop covers 40 acres, and is now operated by the second generation, Kevin and Beverly (Jordan) Childress. Honoring the hard work and memory of James Jordan, Kevin continues as the general manager, Beverly concentrates on the growing process and Ms. Carol still advises in the General Store and Garden Center.

Your entire family will enjoy visiting Jordan's Plant Farm, 7523 State Hwy. 42 S. It is fashioned after an old-timey Western town, complete with general store, post office, grandma's kitchen, hotel lobby and saloon. The original building was purchased from the set of Walt Disney's movie, "The Man Who Broke A 1,000 Chains," where it was used as a hospital barracks. Another room was

purchased from the set of "Long Hot Summer" that was filmed outside of Marshall, Texas. Grab a cup of complimentary coffee while you browse the greenhouses and fun shops or just enjoy the peace and quiet of the country setting in a rocking chair on the front porch. The kiddos will love the old-fashioned candy counter, which is stocked with tasty chocolates, jawbreakers, gummy favorites and stick candy in every flavor.

There are more than 100 plant varieties throughout the property, including bedding plants, vegetables, flowers and special items for each season. Enjoy bright festive flowers in the spring, custom-made wreaths and pumpkins in the fall and a Christmas wonderland during the holiday season. Visit www.jordansplantfarm.com or call 903-854-2316. *(Color photo featured in front section of book.)*

Lorraine White sees things just a little differently than most folks. What might look old and worn out to some becomes something fabulous and trendy in her hands. Her wildly popular store, Plan It Home, is probably the most unique and intriguing "whimsy" in town. Located at 100 N. Marshall St. in downtown Henderson, the beautiful interior design store is filled with one-of-a-kind fabrics and upholstered furniture, vintage rugs and unusual hardware. Lorraine combines her passion for art, antiques and fabrics to help others add color, drama and style to their homes and offices. She says, "I love taking a tired piece of furniture and adding a fresh coat of paint, perhaps some designer tile and quirky hardware and making a statement piece!" She carries a colorful line of wool rugs by Company C and is the East Texas dealer for Faux Iron. Her creations are truly fabulous. Just don't stand still too long in the store. She recycles everything! Visit www.planithome.net or call 903-445-6897.

Donovan's
Downtown Henderson

Starting with little more than a lawn mower, a knack for landscape design, and a portable building, Donovan Dickeson now has a wonderful home and garden gift shop in historic downtown Henderson and a second location seven miles out of town. Donovan's, 112 E. Main St., is located in a wonderful 100-year-old building and is known for its great selection of accessories, accent furniture, and natural looking botanicals and florals. The Shop is also famous for its seasonal Christmas displays. Donovan says, "Clients come from Dallas, Houston and all over Louisiana just to see our holiday treasures."

Donovan started working at a nursery while in college and developed his skills in landscape and interior design. His true talent in finding unique inventory along with his friendly, all-in-the-family staff and incredible customer service has made Donovan's a favorite Henderson shop. Call 903-655-2240.

The Mustard Seed

After selling their antiques in several other malls through the years, Kim and Steve Johnson decided that it was time for Henderson to enjoy a new shopping venue. They opened The Mustard Seed, 128 E. Main St., in an 1890 circa building, which housed the original Beall's department store. This three-story building boast more than 70 vendors who have a very unique style of displaying merchandise and shoppers really enjoy their time in the store. You will recognize items from Stephen Baby, Willow Tree, Jim Shore, Waxing Poetic and Tokyo Milk and Love & Toast, but you'll also love exploring the store's many antiques and collectibles. There is Shabby Chic décor, wrought iron, antique dinnerware and silver, heirloom lace, dollhouses, milk glass and antique Western tack. That's just a teaser! From furniture to gourmet foods, jewelry to toys, The Mustard Seed has a wonderland of treasures to explore. Call 903-392-8288 visit www.mustardseedshoppe.com.

Baymont Inn & Suites are known for their "hometown hospitality" everywhere, but add the hands-on service by owners Scott Gibson and Chase Sharp, and your stay here in Henderson will be truly outstanding. Chase is a chef and Le Cordon Bleu graduate who worked at Wauwinet on Nantucket Island (rated fifth best resort in North America). When his longtime friend (and former schoolteacher) Scott decided to get into the hospitality business, Chase joined him in the adventure. Together they built Baymont Inn & Suites, 410 Hwy. 79 S. To keep up with Chase's passion for food, the partners opened the Sundowners Bar & Grill onsite (open for dinner Monday-Saturday). It is well known for its delicious food and great ambiance. The steak at Sundowners was voted "Best Steak in Town" by the Henderson Daily News Readers' Poll.

The three-story hotel is beautifully decorated, with marble floors and outstanding features throughout. It has become a favorite venue for special gatherings and corporate events. Guests enjoy an outdoor pool and fitness center, free high-speed wireless Internet service and a business center with 1,000 square feet of meeting space. A hot breakfast of eggs, sausage, waffles, and biscuits and gravy is served each morning. The handsome rooms include 32" flat-panel televisions, coffee makers, hair dryers, microwaves, refrigerators and irons. The Baymont Inn & Suites is the perfect place for your corporate needs, but can also be an incredible home-away-from-home while exploring East Texas. It is "elegance," with a dose of good ole' Southern hospitality and I enjoyed my stay each and every time! For reservations or more information, call 903-657-7900 or visit www.baymontinns.com/hotel/19647.

LONDON MUSEUM & TEA ROOM

On March 18, 1937, the town of New London suffered an incomprehensible loss with the tragic explosion of the local school. Of the 500 students, grades 5-12, and 40 teachers in the school's sleek, modern building, 298 were killed in an explosion that was heard almost four miles away. "Only 130 students escaped serious injury. Workers from around Texas, Louisiana and Arkansas worked for 17 hours, through rain, to rescue every last victim." In memory of the ones who perished and those who survived, the London Museum was established. It continues to commemorate "The Day A Generation Died." Located at 690 S. Main St., the Museum has grown from a humble beginning to a noteworthy presence in the community, with a monument listing the names of the lost, and an impressive collection of data and historical tributes. The Museum now includes a wonderful little Tea Room and an old-fashioned soda fountain where visitors can enjoy a frosty root beer, banana split or ice cream sundae at the fountain, or have one of the delicious lunch specials, homemade soups, great sandwiches or yummy desserts. For hours or information, visit www.newlondonschool.org or call 903-895-4602.

DEPOT MUSEUM
HENDERSON, TEXAS

Get your ticket to the Depot Museum in Henderson and enjoy an exciting, interactive glimpse into East Texas Heritage. Clustered on five acres at 514 N. High St. 12 restored structures give visitors a glimpse into the early life of Rusk County. Native Americans, early Texas settlers and oil hungry wildcatters all helped shape the area, and their influence is still felt today. Open year round, the Museum contains the T.J. Walling Cabin (circa 1841), the Beall-Ross Home (circa 1884), the Missouri Pacific Depot (circa 1901), a Cotton Gin and so much more. The most well-known event of the year (and so much fun!) is the Heritage Syrup Festival, held annually the 2nd Saturday of November. Visitors will love watching the old-time syrup making demonstration—using mule-powered equipment, an antique tractor show, great Folk Arts and crafts, as well as enjoying live musical entertainment. Call 903-657-4303 or visit www.depotmuseum.com.

Howard-Dickinson House

An absolute "must" is the stately Howard-Dickinson House, 501 S. Main St. in Henderson. Perched on a lovely hill at the edge of downtown, the beautiful home stands as testimony to more than 150 years of history and Texas hospitality. Built in 1855 by brothers Dave and Logan Howard, it was occupied by the Howard family for 50 years. Sam Houston, a cousin to Mrs. Martha Howard, was a frequent guest. In the first half of the 20th century the house was occupied by the Dickinsons, during which it was used as a boarding house. By 1950 the home was abandoned and had fallen into ruin, but a decade later the Rusk County Heritage Association had been formed to save it. In 1967 the beautifully restored home opened in its present state. Depicting the lifestyle of a wealthy family of the late 19th century, the home is available for tours or catered luncheons and events. Don't be surprised if you get a visit from the "resident ghost!" Call the Henderson Chamber at 903-657-5528 or visit www.hendersontx.us.

Salons, Spas & Indulgence

What a wonderful place to spend a day being pampered... or at least half a day! Thanks to Rachelle Thrasher, the ladies of Henderson now have a wonderful salon, spa and gift boutique where they can enjoy therapeutic services that treat the body and heal the spirit. Foxx III Salon and Spa, 119 S. Marshall St., has also been a healing gift for Rachelle and her two beautiful daughters, Addy and AnnMarie. Rachelle's husband Clint was a pilot for the Air and Marine Border Patrol. Unfortunately, his plane went down and he was killed in the line of duty. After his death, she moved her children back to her hometown and eventually found a way to do something she loved while taking care of her girls. She and the girls chose the name Foxx III for the salon because it was Clint's designated call sign as a pilot, so it holds special meaning for them and the townspeople. Enjoy full spa and salon services, relax at the coffee bar and visit often to see the unique selection of great fashions and special gifts. Call 903-657-2297.

Special Events, Groups & Corporate

On a picturesque slope overlooking Lake Forest Park, the Henderson Civic Center, 1005 State Hwy. 64 West, is surrounded by a beautifully wooded landscape and small lake. The 19,000-square-feet facility, which has hosted visitors to business conferences, trade shows, banquets, luncheons and receptions, has been a huge benefit, and source of pride for the citizens of Henderson. The Civic Center was a dream 30 years in the making. Many of its rooms are named in honor of local citizens who were dedicated to or made important contributions to the community. Facilities include a stunning reception room with a great view of the lake, a civic hall for large groups, a business conference room and a state-of-the-art kitchen. From small birthday luncheons to huge corporate trade shows, it is the perfect venue. Call 903-392-8232 or visit www.hendersontx.us for more information.

Discover Kilgore

Gushers, high-kickers and "To Be or Not To Be!" All this and more found in the city with a big history that blends its rich oil heritage with an exciting variety of attractions and entertainment. You will, as they say, "strike it rich" in Kilgore, perhaps not with oil, but with fun, excitement and adventure for the entire family. Kilgore was voted by the 78th Texas Legislature as the "City of Stars" because of the many stellar citizens that have grown up in Kilgore and come to shine as stars in the entertainment and public world. A galaxy of stars awaits visitors to Kilgore who simply cast their eyes upon the star-topped derricks that highlight the Kilgore skyline. Kilgore is a place that shines year round and you will love experiencing all that Kilgore offers!

World's Richest Acre

Although plantation owners settled the area before the Civil War, Kilgore was actually founded in 1872 when the city's namesake, Constantine Buckley Kilgore sold the 174-acre town site to the International-Great Northern Railroad. A post office was established by 1873, and by 1885, the population had reached 250. It prospered through the decades like most small, rural towns in East

Texas but was dealt a severe blow with the decline in cotton prices and the Great Depression. Businesses had begun to fold, and Kilgore was nearly a ghost town with a population of only 500. The town's fortune (along with that of much of East Texas) changed forever on October 3, 1930—a date that put the tiny rural town of Kilgore on the map and thrust it into the national spotlight. Wildcatter Columbus M. "Dad" Joiner struck oil just south of town, marking the discovery of the huge East Texas Oilfield. With this discovery of one of the greatest oil fields of all times, Kilgore was transformed into a bustling boomtown almost overnight. In just ten days from the discovery, the town's population exploded to more than 10,000 as fortune seekers from across the country swarmed the town.

By 1939, there were 1,200 oil derricks within the Kilgore city limits—many concentrated within a square-downtown block. In fact, one well was actually drilled right through the floor of the Kilgore National Bank. This section of Kilgore's downtown became known as "The World's Richest Acre," and the city as the capital of the East Texas Oil Field. As you can imagine, this instant fame and growth brought many changes to Kilgore, some unexpected and troublesome. Law enforcement struggled to maintain control with the frenzied population explosion, and in 1931, the state sent legendary Texas Ranger Manuel T. (Lone Wolf) Gonzaullas to help restore order to the city. When the oil boom began to subside, the small oil companies and wildcatters sold out to large corporations, and the town settled back again into a quiet, East Texas rhythm.

More than 80 oil derricks still dot Kilgore's skyline today, and are all topped with stars that are lit during the holiday season. They remain a tribute to Kilgore's oil boom days, and to the contribution that the East Texas oil made to the U.S. Victory in World War II. The **East Texas Oil Museum**, which is located on the Kilgore College campus, explores every aspect of life in the 'oil patch' in a full-size replica of BOOMTOWN, USA. Grab your hardhat and find out what the oil pioneers discovered long ago. You can experience a real gusher, talk with a derrick hand, see and feel the equipment displays, geological exhibits, and even take a (simulated) ride in an elevator 3,800 feet down to the oil formation deep within the earth. Visitors from around the world have visited the museum, which is now one of the leading destinations for tourists in Kilgore.

Thursdays and Fridays "In The Patch"

While the pumping of oil from the many downtown derricks was music to the ears of Kilgore citizens, there is a different beat "in the patch" today. Every Thursday from May through November and Friday from April through August, the Kilgore Historical Preservation Foundation, features free concerts under the derricks. From Country Western and Rock 'n' Roll, to Bluegrass and Jazz—musicians perform under the famous derricks to folks watching from lawn chairs or blankets.

Kicking It Up in Kilgore

If you've watched championship football games or the Macy's Thanksgiving Day Parade, or read *Newsweek, Esquire* or *Texas Monthly* magazines, you're probably familiar with the famous **Kilgore College Rangerettes**. If you're a native Texan, their legendary white hats, cowboy boots and high kicks have been part of your history for more than 60 years. The world-famous Rangerettes took the football field for the first time in 1940, pioneering the field of dancing drill teams so prominent in the country today. They were the creation of Miss Gussie Nell Davis, who was invited to the college by College Dean, Dr. B.E. Masters. He believed the school needed an organization that would attract more young women and "keep people in their seats during football game halftimes." From the moment the beautiful "red, white and blue" dance team strutted out onto the field, they captured the hearts of Texas and the entire country with their bright smiles, enthusiasm and world-famous High Kick Routine. The world's best-known collegiate drill team has traveled from coast to coast and throughout the world, performing in Venezuela, Hong Kong, Korea, France, Singapore and Ireland. They have performed in Washington D.C. at inauguration celebrations for Presidents George W. Bush and Barak Obama, and delighted the hearts of millions who have watched them perform at the New Year's Cotton Bowl Classic each year since 1951.

Share in Kilgore's pride in their famous "star" attraction with a visit to the **Rangerette Showcase and Museum**, located on the Kilgore College campus. Displays of props, costumes and thousands of photographs and newspaper clippings showcase the excitement of this famous team through the years. You can even watch performances by the high-kickers on a large screen in the 60-seat theater. Or, if you happen to be visiting during April, be sure to see them live in their annual variety show called Rangerette Revels.

Wherefore Art Thou Romeo?

Romeo is in Kilgore! Since 1986, Kilgore has hosted *The Texas Shakespeare Festival,* which began as a summer theatre opportunity for professional local, regional and national theatre artists. It has been so successful through the years that it is recognized as one of the leading Shakespeare festivals in the country. Sold out performances are held each summer in the Van Cliburn Auditorium on the Kilgore College campus. Audiences are delighted with an outstanding revolving repertory. It has become a strong and vital asset for all of East Texas. It's definitely *not* "Much Ado About Nothing!"

The City of Stars

Kilgore's rich oil heritage certainly shaped the future of this small, charming city. The city has grown into its own through the years, with a stage of outstanding recreational outdoor and cultural opportunities. The people of Kilgore continue working hard to make Kilgore shine as brightly as the stars atop the downtown derricks. They are attracting new businesses and entertainment venues to the city, encouraging renovation and restoration of old buildings and organizing events like regular Farmer's Markets, Christmas celebrations and Monthly concerts. It has proven the success of the "dominoe" concept; when one business spruces up its facade and becomes successful, others will follow. The city has seen this happen after the opening of the incredibly successful design center, **Two 0 Five**. Interior designer Harry Crouse completely renovated a downtown building into a remarkable full-service design center, adding beautiful loft apartments on the second floor. Its success prompted numerous upscale shops and restaurants to follow suit, resulting in a shopping district that is now a destination for discriminating shoppers from larger cities like Dallas and Houston. Come discover the shining, star-studded city of Kilgore, Texas! *(Color photo featured in front section of book.)*

For more information, call the Kilgore Chamber of Commerce & Visitors Bureau at 903-984-5022, 866-984-0400 or visit www.kilgorechamber.com.

Kilgore
Fairs Festivals & Fun

March
> Lone Star Lug Nuts Car Show

April
> Rangerette Revels
> Spring Film Festival
> Taste, Trade & Music Fest

June
> Texas Shakespeare Festival

July
> Texas Shakespeare Festival

September
> Fall Film Festival
> Danville Maize

October
> Kilgore Night Out
> Downtown Trick-or-Treat
> Danville Maize

November
> Christmas in the Oil Patch
> Mingle & Jingle
> East Texas Oilman's Chili Cook-Off
> Christmas Parade

December
> Holiday Happenings in Historic Homes
> Mt. Kilgore Snow Hill Festival

TWO 0 FIVE

Seasoned interior designer Harry J. Crouse was first introduced to Kilgore ten years ago, and has since played an integral part in developing the town into an exciting shopping destination. He opened Two 0 Five, 205 N. Kilgore St., an incredible, full-service design center with more than 10,000-square-feet of showroom space. Harry completely renovated the downtown building, adding upscale loft apartments on the second floor, and even acquiring and expanding into the adjacent building. Two 0 Five was the first business of its kind in Kilgore, but because of its enormous success, numerous upscale shops and restaurants have opened. Harry and Manager Justin DuPont shop extensively to find truly unique items. They represent some of the finest manufacturers of upholstery, case goods, lighting and accessories. You'll find remarkable furniture and fine art, stunning chandeliers and sconces, beautiful mirrors and tabletop décor. Visit www.shop205.com or call 903-984-4710.

Sally Morton Beane and Barton (Bart) Crowley grew up in Kilgore, both from pioneer families who settled the area during the early 1850s and played an important part in the area's early growth and development. Ultimately it was this history that brought them both back to Kilgore with a desire to revive their hometown. The resulting partnership has built one of the finest antique and design stores in Texas.

With Sally's background in interior design and business management and Bart's experience in both interior and landscape design, a store like Barton & Beane was a natural fit for their talents. It is a rich collection of exquisite American and European antiques, lush rugs, unique lighting and beautiful jewelry from designers around the world. The building, 101 N. Kilgore St., is an antique treasure itself. Built during the oil boom of the 1930s, the space has housed many businesses throughout the years, including a beauty salon, a Hallmark Store, an office supply center and finally an antique store more befitting its history. Layers of old sheetrock, dropped ceilings, fluorescent lighting and false walls were removed to reveal the store's lovely old brick, high ceilings and timeless character. It is filled with beautiful items for the home—grand antiques, dazzling chandeliers, ornate mirrors, fine paintings, lithographs and unusual accessories that will truly define the style of your home. Sally and Bart's fresh approach to home décor and their ever-changing inventory of fine treasures from around the world give their customers

and clients exciting new options each time they visit. Together, with their in-house sales team of designers, they bring an unusual combination of talents to complete the interior décor as well as the exterior landscape of any home or business. Visit www.bartonandbeane.com or call 903-986-3600.

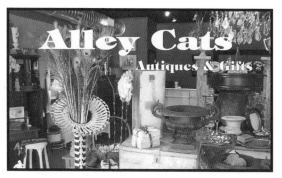

Edgy, fun and eclectic aren't words usually used to describe antiques, but with one trip to Alley Cats Antiques & Gifts, you'll understand why they fit this shop perfectly. Owners David Reeves and Art Martine have collected and worked in the antique business for years, having been involved in the Round Top Antique Fair, as well as dealers in various mall locations. "We both grew up surrounded by antiques," David says, "I can remember being taken to Canton First Mondays as a young child in the 60s. It's just in the blood!" The pair was thrilled when the space at 213 E. Main St. became available, and jumped at the chance to open their own store. The 1926 building, with its interesting art deco details, is one of Kilgore's original downtown structures. It's the perfect backdrop for Alley Cats' unusual treasures, architectural remnants, Shabby Chic items and lots of silver. You'll also find wonderful vintage pottery. Call 903-984-9840 or visit www.alleycatsantiques.net.

RANGERETTE SHOWCASE MUSEUM
& KILGORE COLLEGE RANGERETTES

Called "The Most Sought-after Collegiate Performers in the World," the Kilgore Rangerettes are legendary for their white boots and hats, precision high kicks and brilliant smiles! They have entertained at US presidential inaugurations and traveled the world to exotic places like Hong Kong, Venezuela, Macao, Japan and Ireland. And, in 1977, the squad even spent 15 days behind the Iron Curtain touring in Romania. The Rangerettes began in 1939 when Kilgore College Dean Dr. B. E. Masters decided that the college needed an organization that would attract young women, and keep people in their seats during halftimes (instead of sipping improper beverages under them). In 1940, he brought in Miss Gussie Nell Davis to organize the Kilgore Rangerettes. She is credited with "bringing show business to the gridiron."

The Rangerette Showcase and Museum is located at 1100 Broadway Blvd. on the Kilgore College campus. Watch famed Rangerette performances, and see photos and mementoes of the celebrated high-kickers that pioneered dancing drill teams now seen across the nation. Visit www.rangerette.com or www.kilgore.edu, call the Museum at 903-983-8265 or the Rangerette office at 903-983-8273.

Now-famous oil wildcatter Columbus "Dad" Joiner spudded a hole on the Daisy Bradford farm in Rusk County in 1929, drastically changing the history of East Texas. That single event ushered in an "oil boom" that will never be forgotten. This incredible oil discovery brought thousands of people to Kilgore during the 1930s and almost 1,200 wells were drilled. In fact, the "World's Richest Acre Park" at the corner of Commerce and Main Streets, recreates the literal forest of derricks. Fifty years after the first oil gusher blew in, the multi-million dollar East Texas Oil Museum opened at Kilgore College in 1980. This landmark continues to pay tribute to the independent oilmen that pioneered the discovery and development of the giant oil field.

The Museum was the vision of Mrs. Al G. Hill, Sr. (the eldest daughter of the late H. L. Hunt, a key figure in the East Texas Oil Field). Since it's opening, the Museum has hosted more than 1,350,000 visitors from around the world, and is visited annually by more than 10,000 schoolchildren. The fascinating museum houses an authentic recreation of oil discovery and production during the

1930s. "Boomtown, USA" is a full-scale town of stores, people and machinery that depicts the activity of a town "booming" with oil. There is a general store, a newspaper office, barbershop, blacksmith shop, gas station and theater, where you will see historical footage of the boom period and sense a blowout gusher. You can even take a simulated 3,800-foot elevator ride "to the center of the earth" for an explanation of how oil deposits are found and brought to the surface. The East Texas Oil Museum is located at 1301 Henderson Blvd. S. (at the corner of Ross Street) on the Kilgore Campus. This is a true treasure for the area and a must see on everyone's agenda. Call 903-983-8295 or visit www.easttexasoilmuseum.com.

Fashion, Accessories, Gifts & Home Décor

HEART TO HEART TREASURES

BEST LITTLE GIFT SHOP IN EAST TEXAS

Yellow Box Shoes, Big Star Jeans, fabulous jewelry, home décor, and so much more in one of the most charming little boutiques you'll ever visit. Heart to Heart Treasures, 113 N. Kilgore St., is itself one of the city's greatest "treasures." It is located in historical downtown Kilgore in what was once called "the world's richest acre" because of the large concentration of oil derricks. Owner Anita Ables says that her customers' satisfaction is her top priority. The minute they walk through the door they are greeted with a friendly welcome, a relaxed atmosphere and sincere desire to see them looking and feeling their best. Whether you are looking for the latest in fashion trends, a perfect accessory for an outfit or even a wonderful gift for someone special, Heart to Heart Treasures has it. Anita believes, "It's a fun, comfortable place for some good ole' 'retail therapy.' and …With God, All Things Are Possible!" Call 903-983-7700.

Expressions

♔

Cards & Gifts

You'll recognize the distinctive aroma of one of the ever-popular Tyler candles the minute you walk through the door of this remarkable and beautiful gift store. Expressions, 104 N. Kilgore St. in Kilgore, is a one-stop shop for wonderful items for the home and garden, home fragrances and body products and special gifts. Owners Carl and Coleen Clower invite customers to browse the ever-changing displays throughout their enticing shop. The original store opened in 1977 as Margie's Hallmark, and the Clowers were frequent visitors before purchasing it and moving it to its present location on Kilgore Street. The store now has a delightful flair and charm that attests to Carl's outstanding talent for decorating and interior design. Carl says, "I absolutely love the store, and being able to decorate for my customers is the icing on the cake!" It is his passion, which he says comes second only to his family.

The Clowers pride themselves on being able to find the newest and most-unique items for their customers, and staying ahead of the large market shows. Besides the wonderful Tyler Candles, you'll love the line of vintage-style jewelry called Sweet Romance, and the Jimmy Crystal sunglasses and readers with over-the-top bling! Expressions is also a distributor of the popular Thymes bath and body products.

Longtime customers say that the outstanding personal service offered by the Clowers has made it a local favorite for many years. They know they will always find something they can't live without each time they visit, and can count on Carl to help them with all of their interior design needs. He has the ability to tailor his design work to the individual tastes and budgets of his clients, and the result is happy, faithful customers and new friends. Call 903-984-4113 for more information.

J&Co. is a delightful collaboration between four friends: Jean and Owen Therneau and sisters, Carrie Jackson and Julie Beck. Together they opened J&Co., 120 N. Kilgore St., in November 2008. The foursome met while attending antique shows around Texas. They soon discovered that the Therneaus' love of oriental antiques blended well with the sisters' love of antique and estate jewelry. The delightfully popular J&Co. was born.

This enticing shop carries a wonderful selection of diverse items—both new and old—for all ages. It offers fragrant luxuries from Jack Black and Billy Jealousy for him and Lady Primerose, Hillhouse Naturals, Lollia and Tokoyo milk for her and baby. Antique and estate jewelry as well as fashion jewelry are in abundance. And, if you have trouble making up your mind, J&Co. offers interchangeable jewelry by Kameleon and Scooples. The store's extensive selection of scarfs and hand bags celebrates the vibrant trendsetters in all of us. The Pouchee purse organizer is a must have.

If you need something for baby, J&Co. is your store! It offers clothes by Kissy Kissy, Haute Baby and Baby Bella Maya—newborn necessities are also available. There are also great toys to choose from—both fun and educational.

And, J&Co. hasn't forgotten the gourmet. For those who love to cook and entertain, J&Co. offers delicious dip mixes, brie bakers and tagine cookers from Morocco. There's also an array of items—from china and crystal to sterling silver flatware and serving pieces—to help you entertain with ease and make your time in the kitchen more enjoyable.

With something for everyone, J&Co. should not to be missed. Call 903-984-1420.

CALAMITY JANE'S

Horse tack, cowboy boots and glitz—you'll find it all at Calamity Jane's, 310 S. Kilgore St., a wonderful boutique that is as clever as its name. Owners Patsy and Gary Wayne Davis were born and raised in Kilgore. They know everyone in town, and are very involved with the downtown business community. Their unique Western boutique is located in a historic 1930s building that once served as a dry cleaner, domino hall, restaurant, junk shop and even a home. Today, you'll find a wonderful selection of fun Western wear, handmade and vintage cowboy (and cowgirl) boots, hats, belts, purses and spectacular jewelry for any occasion. (Everyone needs a little "Calamity" in their life and wardrobe!) Patsy makes custom jewelry and can customize anything from shirts to cowboy hats. She says, "I can add 'bling' to just about anything!" You'll love her flair, and you will love Calamity Jane's. Call 903-984-1916.

Florists & Specialty Shops

MAIN STREET *Flowers* and *More*

Martha Fertitta must be the busiest woman we've ever met, and she's surely one of the nicest. With four kids in school, she managed a Kwik Kopy printing business that she started in 1981. Then in 1998 she added Package Plus for packing and shipping. In 2009, she moved to the building across the street which housed a flower and trophy shop that had been a Kilgore favorite for 30 years. She moved the Package Plus business under the same roof with the other two and named it Main Street Flowers and More. Whew! Located at 212 E. Main St. in the original Duncan's 5 & 10, Main Street Flowers and More is a one-stop shop for… well, almost anything you need. Fresh cut flower arrangements, live plants and beautiful silk arrangements are designed in-house and delivered locally. You can order trophies for your group, have a gift engraved, ship a package or even pay an electric bill. Martha has a wonderful team who believe that great customer service is the most important item in the store. Visit www.kilgoreflorist.com or call 903-983-2320.

Hotels & Inns

COMFORT SUITES

OF KILGORE

With amenities like granite countertops, flat-screen televisions, upscale furnishings and luxurious bedding, it's easy to see why the Comfort Suites of Kilgore was awarded the prestigious "2011 Gold Hospitality Award" from Choice Hotels International and voted "Best of the Best 2011" in the Hotel category by the citizens of Kilgore. Owner Rohena Patel and her staff are committed to providing outstanding customer service in this all-suite hotel.

Comfort Suites, 1210 Hwy. 259 N., is located near Kilgore's historic downtown, making it the perfect location for business travelers and visiting families. The handicap-accessible inn features an indoor swimming pool; a state-of-the-art fitness center; a large meeting room and free Wi-Fi. (The lobby has an amazing water feature you just have to see!) Complimentary breakfast is served daily, and Chili's is located on site.

Rohena supports the community by hosting events like the annual Whataburger Antique Car Show and by supporting the local Boys and Girls Club and the Kilgore Crises Center. Call 903-984-2385, 800-4Choice, or visit www.choicehotels.com.

"Nanny Goat" was a term of endearment Sissy Dupre used for her daughter Nancy when she was little. Well, everyone calls her that now, and loves everything about her wonderful Nanny Goat's Café & Feed Bin, 103 N. Kilgore St. Nancy has been in the restaurant business for more than 20 years, from Dallas to Florida and back again to Kilgore's renovated downtown. The restaurant is a family endeavor. Nancy says, "My mother's name, Sissy Dupre, brings a lot of folks in. Our delicious home-style food and friendly ambience keep them coming back for seconds! My brother Larry is always hootin' and hollerin' up front with the customers, while my daughter Jessica and I are cookin' up a storm in the back." Everything is delicious. They can never make enough of their famous Strawberry Pie! You will love this incredible Kilgore café. For more information, call 903-988-8000 or visit www.nannygoatscafe.com.

When folks in Kilgore are hungry for a perfect, juicy hamburger, and crispy, seasoned onion rings, they think of a restaurant that has been part of the community since the 1950s. The Char-Burger Stockade, 206 N. Kilgore St., has maintained its incredible reputation through the decades as a go-to place for great burgers and fries and friendly customer service. Locals will remember with fondness the previous owner, "Mrs. Barbee," who used the honor system because she was usually too busy to do everything. She left a box at the front of the store, where everyone paid their bill and made their own change! The present owners, brother and sister team, Johnny and Karen Wade still use Mrs. Barbee's recipes and carry on her tradition for small-town hospitality and excellent customer service.

Johnny started his own business at the young age of 16 when he opened Ozarks Fried Chicken. Over the years, he's learned the importance and results of hard work and great service to his customers. He is also very proud of the quality of Char-Burger's meat. They get it daily from the local Clower's Meat Market. (The Clowers are the parents of Carl Clower, who owns the wonderful shop in town called Expressions.) Kilgore is a close-knit community,

The luncheon are, from left, Lucille Gilbert, Yvonne Farrar, and Aldeen Barbee, owner and manager.

and the business owners really support each other. Two of Karen's three daughters also join in the fun of the restaurant, making it a multi-generation affair. One does the bookkeeping and the other helps with the daily operations.

What's the Char-Burger's best-seller? All of the Wades say it is their #3 Chili Burger with hand-dipped onion rings. Yum! Everything here is cooked to order, and everything is delicious! They even have a drive-thru. Call 903-984-7646 for hours and information.

It's a place where locals gather to enjoy live music, dig into old-fashioned burgers and fries and catch up on each other's lives. The Back Porch, 904 Broadway Blvd., is a Kilgore tradition—a legend built with love by Vicki and Jackie Clayton. The Claytons have owned The Back Porch since 1990, but its history dates back to the 1960s when it was a pool hall owned by the late Harry Crow. Born and raised in Kilgore, Vicki and Jackie love serving their community, as evidenced in the great service they give to their customers. They are open for breakfast, lunch and dinner, and use only the best meat and freshest ingredients in their dishes. Although famous for their juicy burgers and hand-cut fries, there is a diverse menu, including buffalo. (Ask about the Sue Lou.) They also sell a "Burger Pak," hamburger, bun and all the fixins you can take home and grill yourself. The Back Porch is a Kilgore "must!" Call 903-984-8141.

Pro-Tek Guns

Okay ladies, we've found the perfect place to stash your guys while exploring Kilgore on your *Lady's Day Out!* Pro-Tek Guns, 301 S. Rusk St., is housed in a 1947 building that began as an ice cream manufacturing business, and is the only gun shop within 10 miles. They will love it! And so will you. Owners Frank, Jr. and Jenny Baggett both work in the shop, which is usually full of locals who stop by for a cup of coffee and to swap stories. Frank worked for the Kilgore Police Department for 22 years, as a patrol officer, detective, firearms instructor and city code enforcement officer. Since retiring, he has loved this business, and the opportunity to work as a gunsmith. He says, "The art of a gunsmith is a dying trade, so I have customers who travel from 75 miles away to have their firearms worked on." The Baggetts buy and sell new, used and antique firearms, as well as great accessories and ammunition. It's an interesting place to visit, even for a group of gals and my 15-year-old son was in heaven when we visited! Call 903-983-3409.

Discover Mineola

It's called the "Jewel of East Texas"—a place where whistles still announce the train roaring into town; where nature is "preserved" in a beautiful way; where live theatre is still a choice of entertainment and where fine antiques and a famous burger draw visitors from throughout the state. The locals tout their hometown of Mineola as a place "Where the People Make the Difference." You'll find that to be true during your visit, too.

What's in a Name

Mineola is at the crossing of U.S. 90 and U.S. Hwy. 80. It came into existence in 1873 with the coming of the rail. The Texas and Pacific and the International-Great Northern Railroad (I-GN) actually raced to see which could get there first. It was the I-GN by 15 minutes. And where did the town get its name? According to stories, Major Ira H. Evans, an officer for the I-GN laid out the town site and named it for his daughter, Ola, and a friend, Minnie Patten. Other stories credit Major Rusk, a surveyor for the I-GN for the name.

Mineola established a post office in 1875, and the town incorporated in 1877. With the rail stop there, Mineola grew quickly, and by 1890, the town had seven churches and several schools, hotels and banks. William Jess McDonald, one of the best-known captains of the Texas Rangers, was a storekeeper during the later 1800s and was elected Wood County Sheriff.

Because Mineola was in the heart of East Texas, timber was a major commodity because of its usefulness for railroad tie making and lumber. The early 1900s brought more growth with the coming of a pipeline company and the improvement of the highways, and the discovery of oil in Wood County spurred the economy through the 1940s. Farming was always, and is still a big part of Mineola's personality. It is a rural farm town that has held its own through the depression, World War II and the last decades of the 20th century.

Main Street Mineola

You can spend several days exploring Mineola's historic downtown district. There are wonderful antique shops, clothing boutiques, fun coffee shops, legendary restaurants and cozy bed and breakfasts where you can unwind after a day of shopping. In 1989, Mineola became a designated Texas Main Street City, and in 2000 it was chosen as a National Main Street City by the National Trust for Historic Preservation. Today, it has a strong, focused downtown district, where Main Street is the heart and soul of the community. Old merchants and new ones are committed to revitalizing the historic homes and buildings and establishing Mineola as a great tourist destination. Landmark businesses continue to anchor the town with determination and tradition while new owners bring a burst of energy and flavor into the mix. You'll love it all! And, we have to let you in on this little tip. One of the most dramatic changes made to the historic square was the addition of "period lighting," which really sets Mineola apart from many small communities. Wait around till dusk and see downtown bathed in a beautiful historic glow.

While you're waiting for the lights to come on, enjoy one of the famous burgers and a fried pie from the **East Texas Burger Company** (ETBC), or a cup of warm bread pudding from its sister café next door, **The Waffaletta**. It's rumored that Bonnie and Clyde ordered a burger at ETBC, and they even paid! Both restaurants are first place People's Choice Winners and can accommodate large groups—Red Hatters, knitting clubs or just girlfriends on "A Lady's Day Out!"

All Aboard!

There is an Amtrak stop in Mineola, so a train ride might be a fun experience for your group. Hop off at the Gazebo and start your visit with a tour of the historic train depot, which was restored in 2005 and is home to the **Mineola Railroad Museum**. Kids will love exploring the "Little Red Caboose," which was built in 1973 and donated to the town by the Union Pacific Railroad in 1989.

Now Showing in Mineola!

If you love history and exciting entertainment, take the entire family to a fabulous show at the historic **Select Theater**. Built in 1920, it is the oldest, continuously operated movie theater in Texas, and is designated a Texas Historical Landmark. It is now home to the **Lake Country Playhouse** and Lake Country Orchestra, but also features first-run family movies. Live productions include quality shows like "Man of LaMancha," "The Miracle Worker," "The Foreigner," "Fiddler on the Roof" and "Thoroughly Modern Millie." How historic and how fun!!

The "Natural Side" of Mineola

Outdoor enthusiasts will not want to miss a visit to the **Mineola Nature Preserve**. The city is extremely proud of this new park, which rates within the top 15 in the nation. With 2,900 acres of beautiful land along the Sabine River, the Preserve is one of the largest city-owned parks in the United States. It was developed with a mission to protect the natural wildlife and habitat for generations to come. It is a pristine wetlands environment, and has been designated the "Birding Capital of East Texas." There are more than 193 species of birds that have been observed and identified, critters that crawl, fly and slither, lots of wildlife, longhorn cattle and even buffalo.

Pack a picnic lunch and head for the Nature Preserve's Pavilion and children's playground. There are educational gardens, wildlife viewing areas and miles of hiking and equestrian trails. Take your fishing pole and fish the beautiful Sabine River, or try the stocked pond for the kiddos. Kids (of all ages) will love seeing the active beehive on Johnny Bendy Trail that can be viewed behind safety glass. And don't miss a walk along the abandoned rail bed with historical markers of the early history of Mineola including the days of the Hasiai Tribe of the Caddo Indian Nation. Events during the year include a **Kite Day, Nature Fest and Astronomy Night**.

Play and Stay in Mineola

There is quite a lot to see and do in Mineola. The Preserve can keep you busy for an entire day. Nearby, Lake Fork offers exciting water sports, boating, swimming, skiing, camping adventure and of course fishing. The **Mineola Historical Museum** has 32 exhibits full of memorabilia documenting the town's history. During the day, you can explore great places to shop and dine. At night, you can treat yourself to musical theater, and if you're looking for a restful and luxurious place to stay, you're in luck. Many of Mineola's beautiful, stately historic homes are rated as some of the best bed and breakfasts in Texas. (Guests are treated to Victorian nightshirts, custom coffee by the fire and German pancakes served on fine china at **Munzesheimer Manor B&B**.) Doesn't that sound fabulous?! During the summers, Front Street wakes up bright and early in the morning to the **Mineola Main Street Farmer's Market**, and during the holiday season you can drive just a few miles to Santa Land, or visit Plantation Farms Christmas Tree Farm. There is so much do in Mineola, but it is also a great place to "just do nothing." Relax and enjoy the easy pace of life and friendly chatter of the locals who are always ready with a story if you ask. We know you'll agree that this really is a place where, "People Make the Difference." *(Color photo featured in front section of the book.)*

For additional information, call Mineola Tourism Department at 800-Mineola (664-3652) or visit www.mineola.com.

Mineola Fairs Festivals & Fun

February
Lake Country Playhouse Live performances
Ladies Day Out
Pilot Club Valentine Dinner Dance

March
Mineola Main Street/Amtrak Wine Fest
Lake Country Orchestra Concert

April
Lake Country Playhouse Live performances
Spring Highway 80 Garage Sale
Black and White Bash Dinner Dance benefits Historical Museum

May
National Train Day
May Days Festival
Lake Country Orchestra
Historic Preservation Month
NatureFest

June
Highway 37 Garage Sale

July
Community Fireworks
Mineola Volunteer Fireman Rodeo

League of the Arts Kids Camp
Lake Country Playhouse Live performances
Highway 80 Progressive Car Classic Car Cruise

September
Hay Show

October
Warehouse of Terror
MLOTA Quilt Celebration
N Johnson Gypsy Market Art and Music Festival
Mineola Metric Century "Ride Through the Pines"
Fall Highway 80 Garage Sale
Lake Country Orchestra Fall Concert

November
Iron Horse Fall Fest

December
Annual Christmas events including
Breakfast with Santa
Tour of Homes
Merry Merchants Winter Whirl
Lighted Christmas Parade
Lake Country Orchestra Concert
Santa and Tree Lighting

Antiques

Serendipity   *The knack of making a welcome and unexpected discovery*—that's the definition of serendipity, and it's the perfect name for this antique and collectible haven. Located in a circa 1912 building at 110 S. Johnson St., Serendipity Mall sits on a charming cobblestone street in Mineola's lovely downtown walking district. Even before entering the shop, you are treated to a taste of the treasures you'll find inside when you spy the shop's bright yellow exterior and cross the custom-painted porch (by Denice Calley). Serendipity originally opened as a furniture store in 1999 by Molly and Bill Stuart and Molly's twin sister Dolly Dover. When Dolly passed away in 2002, Molly began leasing out space to vendors. These wonderful people bring even more personality to the shop. One, Linda Wheeler (pictured to the left of Molly), is the wife of the vendor of Twice Blessed, an appropriate name since Linda had a heart transplant in 2008. Whether you love quilts, Western decor, collectibles or stained glass, you'll love discovering Serendipity. Call 903-569-0820

THE BROAD STREET MALL

The Broad Street Mall, 118 E. Broad St., is exactly the type of place you hope to find in the historical district of a small, charming town like Mineola. Antique gliders, wrought iron planters and wheelbarrows filled with pots of flowers outside the front door invite customers to come inside to enjoy displays filled with incredible treasures from the past. Intoxicating candles with popular scents such as Crème Brulee give the store a warm and inviting atmosphere, and the vendors are small-town friendly and helpful. Owner Diana Biggs has been in the antique business since 1989—she first began selling antiques as an outside vendor at First Monday Trade Days in Canton, Texas. She was then able to move to an inside booth at Canton, where she stayed for the next 14 years. Diana says, "I sold furniture, art and lots of smalls, and I loved changing everything often. I specialized in Shabby Chic for a while, and then at one point I began painting lots of things red. I soon became known as 'The Lady with the Red,' and my customers loved coming by each month to see what I had in red. It has always been a fun business."

Now the owner of The Broad Street Mall, Diana, with the help and support of her husband Richard and son Richard Jr., loves sharing the space with others who enjoy her passion for antiques and collectibles. You'll find a little of everything here: primitives, European antiques, vintage jewelry, fine collectibles, books, toys and a selection of The Broad Street Mall Candles (They burn Crème Brulee all day!) You'll love every minute of your visit to this wonderful antique mall. For more information, call 903-569-1686.

Between Friends
ANTIQUES
& Gifts

Friends Donna Hanger and Joyce Moore invite you to a wonderful shopping experience. In 1993, Donna began creating and selling handmade dolls in a local antique shop and quickly became interested in buying and selling antiques. "I went to my first auction and bought a few things, and I was hooked!" she says. Joyce was working in the same shop; they became friends and decided to open their own business and have loved every minute of the experience. When they were presented with the opportunity to relocate and expand, they inherited a fabulous fudge shop in the process! Between Friends, at 114 E. Broad St. in Mineola, is a remarkable collection of primitives, Depression glass, treasures from Europe, as well as trendy gifts and home décor. Browse through their vignettes; then enjoy a homemade cookie or a delicious piece of homemade fudge. Call 903-569-0322 or visit www.mineolafudge.com. *(See related story on page 172.)*

Vintage Charm

Although the unique collectibles and fine antiques are remarkable by themselves, the vintage buildings that house them add an unmistakable "charm" to this store. Vintage Charm, 109 E. Commerce St., is a combination of two historic buildings that are now located across from the depot where they were built in the 1930s. Even though changes have been made, they retain many of the original architectural details like their antique tin ceilings. Owners Beverly and Gerald Guffey connected the buildings with a cut-through, and filled both sides with wonderful antiques, vintage and new fashion jewelry and fabulous home décor and gifts. Beverly and Gerald began their antique business in the 1990s in Oxford, Ala., in an old cotton mill, before moving to Mineola in 1999. They feel right at home here in Mineola's historic downtown district, and have built a great reputation for quality merchandise and superb customer service. Call 903-569-5656.

Cottage Antiques

Anita Peters first developed a passion for fine antiques as a young mother in Vermont. She loved the thrill of searching for a particular treasure and began collecting antiques for herself and friends. Today, she travels throughout the country, especially to the Midwest, for antiques to fill her lovely Mineola store. Fortunately, her son lives in that part of the country, and he and a good friend serve as what she affectionately calls her "Pickers." In 1997, Anita opened Cottage Antiques, 111 E. Broad St., and it has grown into one of the areas most loved and respected antique stores. It is housed in a historic building that used to be a jewelry store, and her aged treasures fit perfectly into the warm space. The store still has the original weighted glass cases that roll up and down, perfect for Anita's stunning displays, especially her displays of antique linens and quilts. You'll find them in almost every part of the store. Anita has them displayed in clever ways that display their wonderful handiwork, and the beautiful ways they can be used today. Call 903-569-5801.

UNIQUES & ANTIQUES

Hurricane Rita blew Melissa Walker from Lake Charles, La. to Mineola and into a new life and career. While trying to decide what to do with her life, she found this wonderful business for sale and said, "Why not?!" It was the best thing she could have done. "My dad used to set up in Canton, so I've been around this 'good used junk' since the 1980s, and I love it!" Uniques & Antiques, 124 S. Line St., is located in what used to be a General Feed Store, and if you look hard enough you can still find seeds between the wooden floor planks. It is now the largest antique mall in Mineola, with more than 45 quality vendors, so the merchandise is constantly changing. Customers love browsing the 8,500-square-foot mall for "uniques and antiques," and especially love the nostalgia of records being played on an old-fashioned record player. Call 903-569-1133.

Dragonfly Art Studio

Sophie Crowson and Melissa Till are a talented mother-daughter-team who left the corporate world, spread their "iridescent" wings and opened the beautiful Dragonfly Art Studio in Mineola. Their only regret? "We didn't do it a long time ago," says Melissa. "After 20 years of creating glass art as a hobby, and talking about it as a business, mom and I stepped out of our comfort zone and are now having the time of our lives." Dragonfly Art Studio, 105 N. Johnson St., is a sparkling collection of glass art: mosaic and garden art, fused glass, glass jewelry, chimes, bottle art and, of course, traditional stained-leaded glass windows and projects. Sophie and Melissa work together on almost every piece, sometimes calling each other in the middle of the night with new ideas. In addition to the studio, they are an integral part of the Mineola Gypsy Market Music & Art Festival that takes place twice a year downtown. Call 903-569-9209.

Founded in 1988 in the back of an old store with chairs borrowed from a nearby church, the Mineola League of the Arts (MLOTA) has grown into a vibrant, cultural asset to the city. Three women walked door to door then, gathering enough interest to charter the organization, which started with 17 members. In 1992, the Meredith Foundation of Mineola provided MLOTA with a grant to purchase the Central Elementary School building, 200 W. Blair St., with a purpose to stimulate and expand community interest and education in the arts, which is achieved through its guild functions and community activities. Now with more than 250 members MLOTA currently supports five guilds—Paint, Fiber/Craft, Quilt, Sculpture, and Line Dance. Each year the League hosts a Fine Art Show, a Quilt Show, and an Art Camp for Children. It provides classes and workshops throughout the year in all areas of artistic interests. MLOTA offers not only classroom settings for learning, but a place for its members to carry on their artistic endeavors. Call 903-569-8877 or visit www.mlota.org.

LAKE COUNTRY PLAYHOUSE
& SELECT THEATER

As one of the oldest, continuously operating movie theaters in Texas, the famous Select Theater, 114 N. Johnson St., is a true Texas (and Mineola) treasure. Mr. and Mrs. R. T. Hooks opened the Theater as a movie house in 1920, and the building retains much of its historical style and ambiance today. In 1978, a group of actors determined to bring live theatre to the Lake Country area formed the Lake Country Playhouse. They purchased the Select in 1993, ensuring that Mineola would continue to have a movie theater and a venue for live theatrical and musical productions. The Playhouse produces four live plays each year—one in each season—and shows first-run movies each weekend. Patrons especially love the summer musicals and popular Christmas shows. The Select is also home to the Lake Country Orchestra (formerly the Wood County Orchestra), which presents four scheduled performances during the year. Call 903-569-2300 or visit www.lakecountryplayhouse.org.

MINEOLA CIVIC CENTER

Located on more than 38 acres in beautiful East Texas, the Mineola Civic Center is a complete convention facility that provides a meeting place for charitable, scientific, literary and educational activities. The Civic Center, 1150 N. Newsome, was made possible by the generous gift of Harrison Wilbert Meredith founder of the Meredith Foundation, in 1958. A truly user-friendly facility, the Center welcomes groups into five large meeting rooms, including the Live Oak Room, a 5,000-square-foot auditorium. It's used for pageants, family and class reunions, training seminars and much more. Its modern, fully staffed kitchen is available for catering events. Since its dedication in 1977, the Center has welcomed

groups from all over Texas and the United States. And, with 224 hookups at the state-of-the-art RV Park, there's always room for RV clubs and rallies. Call 903-569-6115 or visit www.mineola.com. *(See related story page 170.)*

Bed and Breakfasts, Cabins & Cottages

Sip lemonade on the wrap-around porch from old-fashioned jelly glasses; sleep in a Victorian gown or nightshirt; take a bubble bath in an antique claw-foot tub and relish in the luxury of "One of the Top Ten Bed and Breakfasts in Texas!" Your experience at Bob and Sherry Murray's Munzesheimer Manor, 202 N. Newsom St., will be unforgettable. The Murrays purchased the historic Mineola home in 1986, and spent almost an entire year renovating and restoring it. It was built at the turn- of-the-century by German immigrant Gustav Munzesheimer for his new bride, and remains a magnificent testament to our country's Victorian era. There are two parlors, seven fireplaces, many bay windows, and period antiques throughout the home. Four guest rooms and three cottages reflect the area's history during the time of the "Iron Rail." You will be treated like family and leave as friends. The inn has received numerous awards, and the Murrays have been named, "The Friendliest Innkeepers" (in the US). Call 903-569-6634, 888-569-6634 or visit www.munzesheimer.com.

Pine Tree
Bed and Breakfast

Hike, golf, fish, and shop the area. Rest, relax, renew. Sound like heaven? The Pine Tree Bed and Breakfast, 1167 FM 779, is a little slice of East Texas heaven—a private, peaceful country retreat with enough "stretching-out room" for a wonderful, relaxing weekend. Innkeepers Kathy and Mark Bland have always loved staying in bed and breakfasts themselves. So when they decided to open their own, they searched high and low for the perfect place where they could pamper guests the way they love to be pampered. Their journey took them from West Texas to the luscious landscape of Mineola. And on their wedding anniversary, their new B & B was open for business! Now this warm couple cherishes the opportunity to offer

their guests the blessings of a romantic and peaceful stay in one of their three beautiful cottages. Homemade breads and pastries are delivered to your door each morning. It truly is heaven in East Texas! Call 903-768-2474 or visit www.pinetreebandb.com.

Camping & RVing

MINEOLA RV PARK

Mineola is fortunate to have a beautiful Civic Center that provides visitors the opportunity to meet in facilities that are perfect for all types of events. Since its dedication in 1977, the city has added 224 RV hookups, of which 142 have water and electricity. The RV grounds, located at 1150 N. Newsom, include six lighted tennis courts, a wonderful children's playground and a large picnic area. There is also a large pavilion that is perfect for parties. Groups are treated like family at the park and are welcomed with a tray of homemade cookies and true Texas hospitality. If you are fortunate enough to visit during July, be sure to stay for the annual community fireworks—they are spectacular! To plan your next party, reunion or campout, call 903-569-6115 or visit www.mccrvpark.com. *(See related story page 167.)*

It's the only place in Mineola where you can buy a beautiful dress, a fun pair of flip flops, a trendy purse and a fried pie! Ladybug Jungle, 109 E. Broad St., is as fun as its name implies. The store is owned by Shelia Parker and managed by Harla Gray. The two are indeed a dynamic duo. Shelia says that she has been "in retail" or at least "in training" since she was only six weeks old when she rode to the Dallas Farmers' Market on a pillow between her parents. As a young girl she helped her dad sell vegetables at the market to the "city ladies," learning how to display the produce to make it the most appealing. Fast forward a few years and Shelia, who is also a licensed and very busy auctioneer for estate sales and antique auctions, is still having fun in retail with her remarkable ladies' boutique, Ladybug Jungle. "Instead of tomatoes and corn, I'm selling clothes, purses, shoes and jewelry," she says.

Shelia had owned the building that houses Ladybug Jungle as an investment for 14 years. When it came up for lease again, she convinced her friend and retired interior designer, Harla, to help her open the store. Together they have created a place where ladies of all ages can find affordable designer handbags, shoes and accessories to complement any wardrobe. They carry the ever popular Yellow Box shoes, the classic Miche handbag collection, fun and flashy flip flops and Ethyl jeans and jackets with all the "bling" a girl wants. There is also an incredible selection of silver and costume jewelry. And, yes we did say fried pies—flaky and crispy—made from a secret recipe handed down from Shelia's mom. She says, "Purses and pies... what more could a girl want?!" Call 903-569-9820 or visit www.ladybugjungle.com.

Gourmet & Specialty Foods

BETWEEN FRIENDS Fudge

The homemade fudge and cookies are so scrumptious here that folks drive from 150 miles away to get their fill. How about a piece of Chocolate Amaretto Swirl, Triple Trouble or Died and Gone to Heaven? You'll think you are in heaven! Joyce Moore and Donna Hanger cook up batches of decadent homemade fudge and cookies from real butter and the freshest ingredients possible, and the result is some of the best sweet treats in Texas. Between Friends Fudge, 114 E. Broad St. in Mineola, is a must stop for those with a sweet tooth. Donna and Joyce make many different flavors of fudge and cookies, and they are continuously adding more all the time. This sweet shop is located inside Between Friends Antique and Gifts where you'll find incredible antiques and all sorts of unique items. We left with an adorable teapot and a fabulous selection of loose teas. The perfect complement to our fudge and cookies! Call 903-569-0322 or visit www.mineolafudge.com. *(See related story on page 163.)*

Old Country Store

Lee's Old Country Store, 115 S. Johnson St., is just what the name implies. You can pick up a jar of homemade jam or jelly, find a great tasting East Texas wine and even get your boots re-soled in one stop. Owner Lee W. James is well known in Mineola. He volunteers for the sheriff, police and fire departments. But, his love is the Country Store, where he takes pride in offering the most delicious homemade foods made from the freshest ingredients. He learned to cook from his mother as a young child, and always thought his family was wealthy because of the fully stocked pantry of preserved vegetables and fruit. He was also inspired by monthly cooking magazines. "I would take one recipe each month, and make an effort to duplicate the photograph in that issue," he says. Lee's custom-made jams, jellies, salsas, cobblers and quick breads are incredible, and he is often hired to bake large quantities for customers.

Rumor has it that Bonnie and Clyde ate here—and even paid! Experience a delicious taste of Mineola history in the town's oldest eating establishment. The building that now holds **East Texas Burger Company**, 126 E. Broad St., has served the area as a diner since 1907. The Burger Company has been serving locals and celebrities since 1984. In fact, Owners Ken and Debbie Davis say, "Bet your bass you'll love our burgers!" Walk off your meal by visiting **LW Antiques** right next door. Here you can check out all the great antiques and maybe find exactly what you were looking for! Once you have finished antiquing, stop by **LaWaffalata** for a delicious dessert or a delightful lunch. Made famous for its bread pudding and rich cheesecake, it's the perfect place to host a birthday celebration or a meeting of Red Hat Ladies. Both East Texas Burger Company and LaWaffalata have been named the area's 1st Place People's Choice Winners! Visit www.easttexasburger.com or call 903-569-3140.

Kitchens

Whether you need some actual nine-inch nails or have a hankering for a foot-long German sausage, you'll find both here! Customers love browsing through this historic Mineola landmark at 119 E. Broad St. Owner Jim Bittner purchased the deli and hardware store in 2002, continuing the fine Kitchen's reputation as "Texas' Original Hardware/Deli." Of course, the store's history goes back much further, to 1899, in fact, and still has the rope-operated Otis elevator to prove it. Today, in addition to hardware, Kitchen's serves breakfast and lunch daily, but on Friday and Saturday nights it's also a family steakhouse. The Kitchen's menu is extensive, with everything from half-pound burgers, chicken fried steak and "Junkyard Dogs," to lighter fare. Or just grab a seat at the soda fountain for a bowl of Blue Bell ice cream or an authentic "sarsaparilla." It's one stop for "history, hardware or hamburgers!" Call 903-569-2664.

Central Texas

Bryan / College Station

Calvert

Salado

Discover
Bryan/College Station

Bryan/College Station, set in the heart of Central Texas is a community rich in tradition and history, so diverse that you can enjoy a live symphony performance, see a Big 12 Conference football game, take in a real rodeo, enjoy fabulous live bands, visit a renowned art museum and browse wonderful shops and boutiques all in one weekend. It has the exciting amenities of a big city with all the enchanting charm of a small, rural town—and they really do say, "Howdy!"

Early History

Like many mid-19th Century Texas towns, Bryan began as a small-town stop along the rail system. Originally called Millican, it was renamed for William Joel Bryan, nephew to Stephen F. Austin, who sold a square-mile tract of land to the railroad directors. The Houston and Texas Central (H&TC) Railroad Co. arrived in this community in 1860, and Bryan soon became a major distribution center for freight and Confederate troops during the Civil War. It eventually became the county seat for Brazos County and was incorporated in 1871. In the late 1800s, many German, Czech and Italian immigrants began settling the Brazos River Valley, and a large agricultural business developed including the export of cotton, grain, oil, livestock and wool. More than anything else though, the town of Bryan benefited most from the opening of the **Texas Agricultural and Mechanical College (Texas A&M)** in 1876, just four miles outside of the city.

Bryan continued to flourish during the early 1900s, mainly because of the rich agricultural farmlands and strong industrial development. A movement toward downtown revitalization began during the late 1980s, and in 1992, Bryan became a Texas Main Street City. The city has been slowly implementing the "Downtown Bryan Master Plan," revitalizing block by block with new streetscapes and renovated multi-use buildings. You will see a downtown that has returned to its charm of yesteryear with upscale amenities that make it a fun place to play and live. Bryan is today, a vital and energetic community with a population of almost 67,000 citizens who are fiercely proud of their history and the exciting future of their little, big city.

Gig'em

College Station, the actual home to Texas A&M University (TAMU), owes its name and existence to the school's location along a railroad. The university is a triple destination as a Land, Sea and Space Grant institution with projects funded by agencies such as NASA, The National Science Foundation, The National Institutes of Health and the Office of Naval Research. *MoneyMagazine* named College Station the "11th most educated city in the United States." And, it's Aggieland! Until 1960, this incredible university had a strict rule of "No Girls Allowed!" A few girls were allowed to attend classes with the onset of the Great Depression (all daughters of faculty and staff members) but were not allowed to walk the stage for their diploma. The fight for true, equal co-education continued until 1965, and today, women are blazing new paths within the hallowed walls of Texas A&M University.

Bryan/College Station Attractions

You will be amazed at the number of wonderful attractions within the Bryan/College Station area. There are nine museums in Aggieland, including the famous **George H. W. Bush (41st) Presidential Library**, the **Brazos Valley Museum of Natural History** and the **J. Wayne Stark Galleries**, which is located on the Texas A&M campus. Stark was instrumental in bringing museum-quality art onto campus and largely responsible for the success of the Opera and Performing Arts Society in College Station.

Brazos Valley is also becoming a great wine destination, with one winery that has a winemaking history that dates back 200 years! The founders of **Messina Hof** have a winemaking heritage that has been handed down for generations from their homelands of Messina, Sicily and Hof, Germany. (The first-born son of each generation is named Paul and is always the "winemaker!") Their many events through the year include festivals that celebrate wine harvests and grape stomping and of course, the finished product in wonderful wine tastings.

First Fridays in Downtown Bryan /College Station Entertainment

Downtown Bryan comes alive the first Friday of every month when locals and visitors turn out for one great big party. Local artists showcase their treasures, folks line up for romantic carriage rides and incredible live music keeps everything lively and fun. You can stroll from one studio to another to watch live art demonstrations and sample their wares. Enjoy a meal at one of the wonderful downtown restaurants and sip great wines with friends. Three times a year First Fridays are revved into high gear when it becomes "ArtStep." This event has an even greater emphasis on arts and culture with extra performances by live musicians, fine art on display and demonstrations by outstanding artists.

College Station is such a dynamic entertainment venue. Live music is always on the agenda, as well as local theatre, symphonies and Broadway productions. Saturdays are usually reserved for some type of football interaction, and even if you're not lucky enough to have tickets to the game, you can join one of the fun tailgates or crowd in at a sports bars and cheer on the Aggies as a "12th man."

Shop and Dine

We know you will love the spirit of this community, and get caught up in the excitement of just being around such happy people. Aggie Spirit is contagious, and you'll catch it easily. We know you will enjoy all of the cultural activities and recreation opportunities. But we also know the real reason you're on a day out with friends—TO SHOP! Bryan/College Station won't disappoint. Start with the **Old Bryan Marketplace** in downtown Bryan, a beautiful store filled with extraordinary treasures including furniture, antiques, clothing and gifts. Then, make your way through downtown to find other exciting shops like **Jim•n•i** and **Timeless Designs** and many others in both downtown Bryan and College Station. Be sure to make a reservation to dine in one of the city's most wonderful restaurants, **Christopher's World Grill**. Owner "Chef Christopher" traveled the world, working as a chef on private luxury yachts in Europe and the South Pacific before bringing his exciting ideas and recipes back home to Bryan.

Shop, sightsee, feast, play and even stand (the entire time!) and cheer with students at the Texas A&M game. By the end of your visit to Bryan and College Station we guarantee that you too will be surprised at what you've discovered!

For more information, call the Bryan/College Station Convention & Visitors Bureau at 979-280-9898 or visit www.visitaggieland.com.

Bryan / College Station
Fairs Festivals & Fun

January

First Fridays
Martin Luther King
 Celebrations
OPAS Gala

February

First Fridays
Pool Trout Fishout
Texas Independence Day
 Celebrations at Washington-
 On-The-Brazos

March

Armadillo Dash
Big Event
First Fridays

April

Aggie Muster
Art Step
ChiliFest
Duck Jam
Easter Egg Roll & Hunt at The
 George Bush Presidential
 Library & Museum
First Fridays
Parents' Weekend
Run thru the Vines at Messina
 Hof

May

Art Step
BV Symphony Orchestra's
 Derby Day
Children's Festival &
 KIDFISH
First Fridays
Starlight Music Series Begins

June

Art Step
First Fridays
Great American Shootout
 Annual Tournament
Rod Run

July

4th of July Celebration at the
 George Bush Presidential
 Library & Museum
Art Step
First Fridays
Harvest Weekends at Messina
 Hof
PRCA Rodeo

August

Art Step
Feast of Caring
First Fridays
Harvest Weekends at Messina
 Hof
Northgate Music Fest

September

Art Step
Brazos Bluebonnet Quilt
   Guild's Annual Quilt Show
Country Peddler Show
Fiestas Patrias
First Fridays

October

Art Step
Fall Fest & Booseum at the
   Children's Museum
First Fridays
Halloween Murder Mystery
   Dinner at Messina Hof
   Winery
Red Wasp Film Festival
Texas Reds Steak & Grape
   Festival
Texas Renaissance Festival

November

Art Step
First Fridays
Rock the Republic
Santa's Wonderland Opens for
   the Season
Veteran's Day Program at
   Veteran's Memorial Park
Wine Premiere
Worldfest

December

First Fridays
Christmas in the Park at
   Central Park
Holiday Parade
Mulled Wine Weekends at
   Messina Hof
Santa's Wonderland
   open thru December 31st
Papa Noel Tours at Messina
   Hof

Antiques

If you have an obsession with beautiful things, you will absolutely love this beautiful Bryan store. Southern Grace, 102 S. Main St., is filled with enchanting antiques, incredible home décor, vintage style quilts, boutique jewelry and so much more. Owner Lorena Mushinski has created an inviting space filled with incredible things for the home and exquisite gifts that will definitely bring a little "Southern grace" to every home. For many years, she sold to shop owners in Roundtop and Fredericksburg, then decided to open her very own store, first in Bryan and then in Roundtop. Lorena is a creative owner with a great eye for really cool, unusual items like painted scarves and vintage jewelry boxes. From canopied iron beds and beautiful pillows to birdcages and garden items, you are sure to find something wonderful to bring out the romantic in you. The name says it all–Southern Grace, a beautiful, romantic store. Call 979-822-7770.

J. WAYNE STARK GALLERIES
at Texas A&M University

No one person has done more to bring fine art onto the Texas A&M University (TAMU) campus and into the hearts and minds of the students than J. Wayne Stark, for whom the facility was so appropriately named in 1992. Throughout his 33-year career at TAMU, Stark helped bring museum-quality art onto campus and launched a comprehensive visual and performing arts program that continues today. A rigorous criterion for acceptance into the gallery has resulted in an excellent collection of paintings, drawings, photographs and sculpture that focuses on American art of the 19th and 20th centuries, with a strong emphasis on Texas art and artists including Julian Onderdonk, H.O. Kelly, Dorothy Hood and John Biggers. The Stark Galleries also showcases a changing series of traveling exhibitions in the arts and humanities. J. Wayne Stark Galleries is located in the Memorial Student Center. Visit http://uart.tamu.edu or call 979-845-8501.

Established in 1989 as a museum to house the Bill (Class of 1935) and Irma Runyan Art Collection, the MSC Forsyth Center Galleries is one of the Texas A&M University's (TAMU) art museums, with more than 1,200 objects exhibited on a regularly rotating basis. It is located at 110 N. Main St. in downtown Bryan and is open to collectors, scholars and visitors from the seven-county Brazos Valley. The Runyon Collection includes a world-class selection of English Cameo glass, Tiffany and Steuben glass, and an important collection of American paintings. Featured are well-known paintings like *Winding the Clock,* by Winslow Homer and *Cori in Straw Hat,* by Robert Henri. **ART**hursdays feature guest speakers, workshops and art demonstrations and First Fridays in downtown Bryan include a tour of the gallery. For more information and events, call 979-845-9251 or visit www.forsyth.tamu.edu.

Bringing World-Class Entertainment to the Brazos Valley

The arts have always played a huge part in the communities of College Station and Bryan. Celebrating its 40th season in 2012-13, MSC OPAS at Texas A&M University (TAMU) was founded in 1972, to serve as a vehicle for promoting the arts in the Brazos County area. Through the decades, OPAS has continued to present outstanding performances from world-class artists to the students, faculty and residents of the community. OPAS boasts top-name artists like Itzhak Perlman, Marcel Marceau, the Vienna Boys Choir and Yo-Yo Ma. With exciting musicals and plays like *Cats, Les Misérables* and *Mamma Mia!*; OPAS continues to thrill audiences and inspire the support of this great organization. Most performances take place on the TAMU campus in Rudder Auditorium and will include new plays and musicals like *In The Heights, Young Frankenstein, South Pacific* and Blue Man Group. Call 979-845-1234 or visit www.mscopas.org.

What a great idea! Gather friends for a birthday party or a girls' night out and celebrate with fun and creativity. U paint•it, 900 Harvey Rd., is a contemporary paint-your-own-pottery studio. Owners Valerie Woodcock and Penny Woodcock-Bane are a mother-daughter-duo with backgrounds in both early childhood and higher education. They are excited about their endeavor in College Station. They provide a large selection of unfinished bisque, from functional to whimsical, and all you need to create your own masterpiece. You can pre-select the pottery for a themed event, or let each guest choose their own. After the pieces are decorated, they are glazed, fired and ready in six days; they will even ship your masterpiece directly to you. No artistic talent is necessary. And who knows? You may just discover a new hidden talent and passion! For information and reservations, call 979-695-1500 or visit www.upaintit.com.

Long time Brazos Valley residents, Sue and Dennis Corrington saw a need for a shop where others could find the type of treasures they traveled throughout Texas to buy. D & S Premier Art and Clocks is located at 208 N. Bryan Ave. in Bryan's historical Perry Building, which was built in 1921. Originally a feed store, hat shop and the Perry Brothers Five and Dime, it was remodeled into two retail spaces and eight loft apartments, all with the original brick walls. Today, it is home to timeless treasures that the Corringtons hope will pass from generation to generation. There are more than 200 oil paintings in beautiful, ornate frames (many very reasonably priced) and a large selection of

signed and numbered prints by well-known artists like G. Harvey and Robert Summers. The store offers wonderful Howard Miller grandfather, mantel and wall clocks and excellent clock repair service. (They even make house calls.) Call 979-779-2211 or visit www. dspremierartandclocks.com.

Greta Watkins always knew she was a true "artist" at heart, but it wasn't until she went back to school (at 40!) to get her art degree that she discovered her true passion. She opened The Frame Gallery, 216 N. Bryan Ave., and has become integrally involved with historic downtown Bryan. Aside from professional framing services, Greta showcases more than 60 artists with works that include paintings, pottery, glass and jewelry. Her favorite times have become "First Friday" events in downtown Bryan; Greta was instrumental in starting up the event that continues to grow with amazing popularity. Call 979-822-0496 or visit www.framegallerydowntown.com.

Bed and Breakfasts & Cottages

Rudder-Jessup B&B

Owners George and Hillary Jessup offer their guests a delicious helping of Southern hospitality and Aggie history in the historic Rudder Jessup B&B. Built in 1936, the stately two-story Colonial home was purchased by the University for the Earl Rudder family in 1963. Rudder was a highly decorated WWII general and one of the most influential presidents in Texas A&M history. The Jessup family purchased the home in 1982, and completely restored and expanded it in 1999. They now share its beauty and history with their guests. Four elegant guest rooms, with private baths, are furnished with beautiful period pieces and historic memorabilia. The Jessups are exceptional hosts who make their guests feel like they've "come home." George and Hillary prepare a full gourmet breakfast each morning. The B&B is also available for meetings, receptions and retreats. Call 979-693-1749 or visit www.rudderbandb.com. Or, contact Aggie Bed & Breakfast Finder at 866-745-2936 or visit www.aggiebnb.com.

Lisa Ketchum recognized its potential as soon as she saw the property was up for sale. She knew it was perfect for the bed and breakfast she had dreamed of owning. Designed by well-known Bryan architects, this unusual Bryan home at 1015 E. 24th St. is three stories, each one larger than the one below and each with its own private patio or balcony. Lisa's family did all of the renovation work inside and out, turning Abigaile's Treehouse into peaceful suites and Connor's Corner—the lush gardens—into a tranquil sanctuary, both named for Lisa's grandchildren. Each floor has unique suites that provide guests with a serene place to rejuvenate. The first and second floors are wonderful, but the third floor is amazing. The Eagle's Nest—perched in the treetops—takes up the entire floor and features a king-size bed with designer bedding, large

hot tub, resort-style shower, fireplace, reading loft, and wonderful wrap-around balcony. The Robinson Family would have loved it here! Call 979-823-6350 or visit www.abigailestreehouse.com. *(Featured on the front cover and in the front section of book.)*

The Clary House
Bed & Breakfast

Linda Roberts always wanted to own a bed and breakfast. With three Aggie children, she decided that Bryan/College Station would be the perfect location. (She gives them each one free night per year!) She purchased the beautiful, historic home at 601 E. 30th St. from the Clary family who had lived there for more than 40 years. After getting to know the family, she decided that the wonderful inn could only have one name—The Clary House. Southern hospitality is—and has always been—a hallmark here. Its eight gables, antique furnishings, spacious rooms and beautiful stained glass windows invite guests to relax. A charming wraparound porch is perfect for leisurely afternoons or evenings, and an elegant wood staircase leads to three luxurious

guest suites on the second floor. Linda's motto says it all: "Be warm, be welcome, be at home." Call 832-443-7633, 979-703-7916 or visit www.theclaryhouse.com. *(Color photo featured in front section of book.)*

While on a visit to his alma mater in College Station, Jim Butcher took his wife Earlene to downtown Bryan where Earlene says the town "took my heart." They knew immediately that it was the perfect place to retire and open her long-time dream shop. Jim•n•i, 202A W. 26th St., has become a favorite go-to for stunning clothing from lines like Oh My Gauze and Young Essence, beautiful jewelry by Stuart Peterman and Kameleon, scarves, purses and shoes, and lovely home décor. Jim•n•i is a great store with wonderful owners and remarkable selections of fine things. Visit www.jimnishop.com or call 979-823-8000.

Karen Witt Kasper has owned this wonderful College Station boutique since 1991 and is greatly loved and respected in the area. Witt's End, 3525 Longmire Dr., is a beautiful collection of ladies clothing lines, including the popular Ivy Jane and ISDA. Karen grew up in Tyler and worked for a boutique similar to this one. After graduating from Texas A&M . With her mother as a major supporter, Karen opened Witt's End (a clever take on her maiden name). She has loved every minute of the experience. She says, "The store is more than a pretty dress or a great pair of jeans. Our customers have become part of our family, so it's wonderful to help them feel good about how they look and feel." You will love the great selection of beautiful clothes, jewelry and accessories at Witt's End. Visit www.witts-end.com or call 979-485-8991.

Since the doors opened in 1983, Catalena Hatters has continued to garner accolades from Texans who are passionate and particular about their hats. Family-owned-and-operated by Sammy and Carolyn Catalena (and now the second generation of hatters, Scott and Travis), Catalena Hatters has been making quality custom hats with high standards and reasonable prices for nearly 30 years, The Catalenas say, "We make our hats the old-fashioned way—by hand and one at a time."

Sammy and Carolyn always had a strong interest in custom hats, so when they heard about a hatter in Florida that was selling his business they traveled south, bought the machinery and set up shop at 203 N. Main St. in Bryan. Through the years, they have renovated the historic building, exposing wonderful, original elements such as the beautiful limestone walls and concrete floor.

Sammy is also a rancher and is a Stock Contractor for the Professional Rodeo Cowboys Association, so he knows a little about hats. He and Carolyn have worked hard to grow the business through the years, changing with times and trends in Western fashion. They say, "We were the first custom hatter to advertise and sell the "Gus" hat made popular by Robert Duval in Lonesome Dove." They also have a large mail order business, sending hats to almost every continent in the world. Because of their stellar reputation throughout Texas and the entire country, the Catalenas make it a point to work directly with their customers, so they can control the quality and look

of each hat. And, if you just can't bear to give up that dirty, worn-out, favorite hat, Catalena Hatters has an excellent felt hat restoration process that will give it a new look and life. Call 979-822-4423 or visit www.catalenahats.com.

Gifts, Home Décor & Florists

Old Bryan marketplace This is truly is a one-of-a-kind store; a treasure hunters' delight; and a fantastic shopping adventure. The wonderful pine floors, exposed beams, leaded glass doors, beautiful bricked archways and working fireplaces make Old Bryan Marketplace a wonderful place to explore...but that's only part of the charm. It is filled to the brim with extraordinary treasures, furniture, home accessories, gifts, clothing and collectibles. The ever popular Flax and Johnny Was, delicious gourmet food and wonderful candle lines are just the beginning of the find. Owner Kay Conlee is a fourth-generation Bryan native and proud to be an Aggie. Kay and her son Grant make sure your shopping experience at their store is unlike any other. Old Bryan Marketplace, 202 S. Bryan Ave., has become an integral part of historical downtown Bryan's successful revitalization. Call 979-779-3245 or visit www.oldbryan.com

a floral gathering

fresh flowers · weddings · silk flowers · gifts

This remarkable floral and gift store is always filled with beautiful, fresh flowers, floral arrangements and lots of happiness and joy. Tricia Barksdale Designs, 112 Rock Prairie Rd., is a favorite College Station shop where customers are friends. Customers know they will find arrangements and gifts for any occasion as well as a beautiful place to relax, have fun and just "smell the roses." Of course, with Tricia's passion for plants mixed with her education—she holds a Master's degree in Horticulture Therapy from Texas A&M—that's exactly what she was striving for. "In the evenings, it is sometimes used for gatherings such as prayer groups and book studies," she says. "I want this shop to create great memories for lots of people!" You will love Tricia's creativity in combining herbs with flowers and mixing fragrance and texture in unusual containers like antique sugar bowls and teacups. Many of her arrangements are reminiscent of a cottage garden. Call 979-693-5387 or visit www.triciabarksdale.com.

HOTEL

By Magnolia Hotels

This beautiful downtown Bryan hotel has such an incredible, rich history. LaSalle Hotel, 120 S. Main St., originally opened as one of the town's first two-story buildings in 1866. At that time, the first floor was used for retail and the entire second floor housed the Academy of Music, Bryan's first theatre company and opera house. It officially became the LaSalle Hotel in 1928 and was soon known as a social niche for Brazos Valley residents. The historic LaSalle is now owned by the city of Bryan but is managed by the prestigious Magnolia Hotels.

A nationally registered historic landmark, the LaSalle was beautifully renovated in 2000 and is a fabulous boutique hotel. Because of the rich architectural heritage reflected in the fine preservation of the historic building there is a lovely vintage charm about the place that you will sense the moment you walk into the lobby. You will love the traditional quality combined with all of the modern conveniences and unparalleled hospitality that make it such a premier hotel.

You will be treated to a complimentary breakfast each morning and invited to an evening beer and wine reception each evening. They even put you to sleep with a bedtime cookie service—no matter your age! The hotel's signature lounge, The Club, offers guests a swank and sophisticated place with contemporary décor, plush seating and an intimate bar where guests can socialize and relax.

The LaSalle is the perfect choice for both business and leisure travelers. Visit www.lasalle-hotel.com or call 888-915-1110 for reservations.

The Jewelry & Coin Exchange

This store is a wonderful surprise because the name doesn't tell the whole story. Located in the shadow of Texas A&M University at 313 B College Ave., The Jewelry & Coin Exchange is a full-service jewelry store specializing in custom jewelry from top craftsmen and diamond cutters. Here, you'll find exceptional designs at excellent prices. Owner Donna Wall says that people are pleasantly surprised at her quality and prices. She cuts out the middleman and passes the savings on to her smiling customers. Her favorite slogan is, "A diamond lasts forever; paying for it shouldn't."

You'll find everything here from "fun fashion" to a five-carat diamond solitaire and everything in between. If you are a coin or precious metals investor, you will appreciate their collection of thousands of rare coins that sell from $1 to $10,000. There is also a large selection of collectible gold coins, paper money and gold and silver bullion. And, don't leave without visiting the special room in the store called Treasure Gallery, which showcases amazing antique jewelry that people have sold or traded. When you find a piece you love, the onsite jewelers can have it sized and ready for you, usually that same day.

Store manager David Weaver says, "My favorite part of this job is meeting new people every day. We love to welcome new people into our jewelry family." This type of genuine care and customer service is just another thing that makes The Jewelry and Coin Exchange a favorite place to shop. Donna and her entire staff go out of their way to help their customers find just the perfect piece of jewelry in a comfortable and pleasant atmosphere. For more information, call 979-846-2400 or visit www.jewelrycoinexchangebcs.com.

Entering this incredible jewelry and fashion boutique is like stepping into an exotic world of beauty. Boutique Ginny, 1500 Harvey Rd., in Post Oak Mall, is the result of Ginny Gegg's intense passion for travel and adventure, her appreciation for beautiful jewelry and fashion, and her desire to bring these treasures from around the world to others. Her story is delightful!

Ginny says, "One of my life goals was to travel, and during all of my trips I would buy jewelry as a souvenir. Friends seemed fascinated by the jewelry and its origin and story." A friend asked her to buy a piece of jewelry on her next trip, so when she traveled to Egypt, she brought 30 necklaces back and sold them to friends, neighbors and colleagues on the Texas A&M University (TAMU) campus. Everyone loved hearing about the history of the pieces and having the opportunity to buy something unique and special. She realized that this was an opportunity to turn her love of travel and jewelry into a wonderful business.

Ginny's business started at an arts and crafts show with one table of ethnic and exotic jewelry and a money belt around her waist. Everything sold so well that she then opened full time in a Kiosk, at Post Oak Mall, in College Station, and in 2007, she opened the doors of Boutique Ginny inside the mall. Ginny still travels to exotic places to find her jewelry–pearl markets in Shanghai, cinnabar markets in Beijing, jade markets in Hong Kong, amethyst markets of Brazil, Baltic amber markets in Russia and Poland and even the Sahara Desert for tribal designs of the nomadic people. She loves finding what she calls "wearable art" that represents and honors the culture, traditions and religions of the world. Visit www.boutiqueginny.com or call 979-680-1700.

Linda Ezell believes that when something is created by hand with love and care, it becomes a timeless treasure. She began making 14k and sterling jewelry as a hobby, and while selling her creations at art shows, she met other craftsmen with her same passion. In opening Timeless Designs, 103 S. Bryan Ave., she envisioned an enchanting place where she could showcase her unique jewelry while providing others with a place to share their handmade creations, too. She says, "I think handcrafted gifts touch hearts rather than pocketbooks, and having a shop filled with love makes me very happy." You will adore her one-of-a-kind creations and can even watch her work on custom pieces for her faithful fans, while you shop. Other items include a clothing line from Austin, which uniquely flatters all sizes and gourmet pastas made from all natural ingredients. This is a truly a unique showroom filled with wonderful "timeless designs." Call 979-823-1957.

Cool contemporary meets historic downtown in this incredible art café in Bryan. The Village, 210 W. 26th St., is a trendy restaurant, coffee shop, art gallery and entertainment venue all rolled into one. Owner Kristy Petty says she "opened The Village on a wing and a prayer. I didn't want life to pass me by in a cubicle." She dreamed of a place to feature local art. When she found the 100-year-old building, she knew it would be perfect. Kristy serves everything local—local food, local coffee, local music, local art and local beer and wine. "We support the community," she says, "and they support us." The Village is an eclectic mix of café tables and soft seating. Its ever-changing artwork and live music bring new life to the space monthly. Visit www.thevillagedowntown.com or call 979-703-8514.

Discover Calvert

This wonderful little Texas charmer has often been called, "The Place That Time Forgot." It was once the fourth largest city in Texas with a population of more than 10,000. Then after a series of setbacks, it fell into decline and its Main Street was almost completely boarded up. But today, Calvert has hopped right back on the Texas tourism map. It's an up-and-coming community—only a short drive from Bryan/College Station and a stop you shouldn't miss!

Cotton, Railroads, Southern Gentlemen and Wild West Weekends

The town was founded in 1868 and named in honor of Robert Calvert, a plantation owner who was a descendant of Lord Baltimore, the founding father of the State of Maryland. Calvert was instrumental in bringing the railroad through Robertson County. This resulted in new business and prosperity for the small town. Calvert quickly became one of Texas' leading agricultural centers with one of the largest cotton gins in the world. Cotton planters were soon attracted to the developing town, and began building beautiful Victorian mansions, a tribute to their prosperity and Southern roots.

The town's mix of Southern plantation owners and adventurous rail and cotton entrepreneurs provided the town with its incredible architectural heritage. Many of these incredible plantation homes, located within Calvert's downtown historical district, are still standing today. You can pick up a self-guided driving tour book at many of the downtown businesses and step back into Calvert's history. The tour will guide you down the beautiful tree-lined streets with illustrated, detailed information about each site and on one of the historical markers you can read how the Black Chinese were so instrumental in building the railroad in Calvert.

One of the most interesting buildings in downtown Calvert is **The Hammond House**. Originally built as the county jail, the building covers two city blocks and is an incredible example of Texas' early infatuation with Gothic architecture. Ladies, you will also have the opportunity to visit one of Texas' first *American Woman's League (AWL) First Edition Chapter Houses* in Calvert's historic downtown. These chapter houses were built as meeting places for the first women's clubs. Calvert's Chapter House, completed in 1909, was the first of three in Texas, and one of the first four in the country. Sadly, it is the only one left in Texas that is still functioning as a community center. In 1939, it was named *The Katy Hammon Striker Library*. It remains a symbol of women's life during Texas' Progressive Era.

A tour through the beautiful Historic District will give you an idea about what life was like during Calvert's early glory days. The district is divided by a wide, spacious street, which was originally designed large enough to allow a three- or four-team wagon cart filled with cotton, to turn around. Cotton was central to the growth of Calvert, but the city also became a great cultural center, gaining its own opera house and even attracting the Ringling Bros. and Barnum & Bailey Circus. It also gained a rather infamous "Wild West" downtown reputation during the boom days when hard-working men came into town on Saturday nights for "fun!" There were many saloons and gambling establishments, and so many fights and killings that local families wouldn't even venture into town on the weekends.

The late 19th century brought many challenges to the people of Calvert. In 1873, a yellow fever epidemic broke out in the community, killing many citizens. In 1891, a fire burned much of the town's center, and then in 1899, the town was terribly damaged by many floods.

Even after these setbacks and the difficulties of World War II, Calvert continued to grow and prosper through the 40s, 50s and

60s, mainly because of all of the farm labor in the county. Then in the early 1960s, Calvert experienced another setback. With the mechanization of the cotton industry, many workers were out of work. Mom-and-pop stores shut down, and the town began to wither. The 90s brought a short-lived interest in antiques, and for a while, Calvert became an antique destination, but that little streak of success began to fail with the popularity of Internet shopping and mega antique malls. The boomtown that was forged by the railroad and cotton, then suffered decline after World War II, has indeed seen many ups and downs during its history, but new life, energy and talent is being pumped into Calvert that is making it once again a great place to visit and live.

Still Standing

W.D. Spigner Elementary School in Calvert was built under the Rosenwald Rural School Building program. Rosenwald Schools served as a major effort to improve the quality of public education for African Americans in the early 20th Century South. WD Spigner was built in 1929 and is one of a few original Rosenwald School buildings still in use today!

Culture and Chocolate

With a population today of just over 1,300, Calvert is determined to keep its name and place on the map. And, what better way to do it than with *chocolate!* A decade ago, Main Street was on the verge of collapse, but the town remained a beautiful place with friendly, hard-working people. It attracted the attention of chef and entrepreneur Ken Wilkinson, who chose Calvert for the location of his chocolate boutique and restaurant, **Cocoamoda**. Its opening, along with a transforming Main Street has resulted in a community with new growth, new business and a restored sense of Main Street unity.

Today, there is a high-end Western furniture and fashion store, **Cowboy Up** and several art galleries. The old movie theater, **The Eloia**, has re-opened as an antique store, with future plans to show old films and build an old-fashioned soda shop in the lobby. And, after all of the great shopping and history tours, visitors can rejuvenate with a lunch of home-style country comfort food from the **Wooden Spoon** or grab a cup of coffee and a Czech pastry at **Zamykal Kolaches** in downtown. Be sure though, to end up back at the wonderful little chocolate shop that started it all for an indescribable truffle filled with espresso ganache, mint or key lime.

Yellow Biker Man

What in the world is that "Yellow Biker Man?" You can't miss him. For 11 years, the life-size statue has stood right at the corner of Main and Mitchell Streets—a yellow cyclist on a 1972 Schwinn Varsity Road Bike—and he has a great story. (For all of the details, stop in at **Mud Creek Pottery** and talk to owner Sonny Moss, who donated his now-vintage bicycle to the rider.) He asked artist Paula Cloud to create an inspirational greeter for the riders coming through Calvert on an AIDSRide in 1999. The fiberglass and Bondo biker was named "Spirit of the Ride," and was a huge hit for both the riders and the townspeople. The year after the first AIDSRide, Moss painted the biker "yellow" in honor of Lance Armstrong who won the Tour de France. Since then Yellow Biker Man has been a permanent fixture in Calvert. In fact, he could almost be considered a representative of what Moss and the forward-thinking merchants and city leaders hope the future will bring—a "movement" toward prosperity and success. Slowly, but certainly, they are seeing the beginning of an enclave of talented artists in Calvert, who are opening their doors to locals and visitors for instruction and demonstrations. We look forward to Calvert becoming a flourishing destination city for the arts.

From Sop BBQ to High Tea

The key to really discovering the historic beauty and many treasures of Calvert is to take your time. Spend a weekend in one of the fascinating Bed and Breakfasts like the **Parish House** or **Pin Oak.** This slow-going approach will allow you to appreciate the genteel days of yesteryear. Take your group on a relaxing picnic in *Virginia Field Park* (where Civil War heroes held reunions) or "sop" barbecue at the annual **Link Harlan SOP Style BBQ Cookoff**. The Sop-style of barbecue is a continuous basting with a sauce that has a base of vinegar, cola or fruit juice. It was reportedly developed here in Calvert. Great fun!

For all you "ladies" who fancy getting all dressed up, **The Victorian Tea and Gala** is a perfect reason for your visit to Calvert. Considered "The Event of the Year" in Calvert, this Victorian weekend party will definitely take you back in time, with folks dressed in splendid Victorian attire, old fashioned hayrides, story-tellings and historical home tours. Enjoy a sumptuous afternoon "Tea" of home-baked sweet and savory delicacies served by Victorian servers at the historic Gibson-Hensarling Home. Try your hand at English croquet on the lawn, enter a tea hat contest, and tour the restored Victorian cottage on the property. Then get all dressed up for dinner and dancing at the Virginia Field Park Pavilion. You may even win the contest for "Best Victorian Costume!"

Whether you plan to spend your time poking through the art galleries and interesting shops, learning the early history of the downtown district or just enjoying the slow pace of small-town Texas, you will love your visit to Calvert. Enjoy it with a piece of chocolate . . . because you never know what you'll find inside!!!
(Color photo featured in front section of the book.)

For additional information, call Calvert Chamber of Commerce at 979-364-2559 or visit www.calverttx.com.

Calvert
Fairs Festivals & Fun

June
  Harlan SOP Style BBQ Cookoff

September
  The Victorian Tea & Gala

Antiques

HOMESTEAD HOUSE INTERIORS

Husband and wife owners Dennis and Rabecca Joyce have created a beautiful and elegant store filled with wonderful Victorian antiques and home décor. Homestead House Interiors, 515 S. Main St., is located in a lovely historic building that was built in 1877, and is listed on the National Register of Historic Places. Rabecca is a Master Florist with more than 20 years experience. She previously owned a floral business in Sherman. Rebecca still enjoys designing incredible arrangements, and her fabulous floral masterpieces are just one more reason customers love this store. The Joyces are extremely knowledgeable about antiques and furniture refinishing and have an excellent eye for quality. Their interior design services include furniture repair, refinishing and upholstery, as well as, the little finishing touches that will define your unique style. And, the Joyces still find time to be very active in the Calvert community. Call 979-492-6805.

Artists, Art Galleries & Jewelry

A PLACE TO MAKE ART

M.L. "Sonny" Moss is a well-known name throughout the Brazos Valley. He is an acclaimed potter whose works have been featured in the *Texas County Reporter,* on Channel 8 Dallas and in the Dallas Design District. His studio and gallery has become a favorite place for artists and friends to gather, share and learn. Mud Creek Pottery, 419 S. Main St., is located in a circa 1878 building that houses the gallery and studio with a kiln yard behind the building. Next to the studio, an outdoor patio is a peaceful meeting place for artists and friends, and another large studio serves as a teaching facility for students and groups. Sonny offers a wide range of glazed, hand-thrown items, as well as hands-on instruction in wheel-throwing, hand building and "raku." His incredible talent and commitment to art education have been instrumental in making Calvert an exciting "arts destination." Visit www.mudcreekpottery.com or call 979-364-3730, 800-670-8183.

One peek at this charming store, with its elaborate gabled entrance made from lean-to shutters covered with grapevine, birdhouses and wind chimes, and you'll be enticed. Add to that the wonderful scent of hand-poured candles, and you'll be convinced—Common Scents, 605 S. Main St., is an incredible treasure! It's located in a historic 1860 building that serves as both the store and Owner Candy Shores' home. It is filled with Candy's own handcrafted jewelry, as well as other designers, wonderful Shabby Chic décor, Santa Fe-inspired art, cowboy furniture, antiques and collectibles and the most delicious smelling candles. Candy stocks as many as 50 different scents, which she calls "working candles," because one will scent your entire house. She began making the candles out of her home, and giving them away as samples. The demand quickly grew into this amazing store in Calvert's historic downtown. Don't miss it! Visit www.forttumbleweed.net/candy.html or call 979-324-4006.

THE ELOIA

ANTIQUES • DECOR • GIFTS • SWEET SHOP

A beautiful, historic, small-town theater has found a new life! The Eloia, 504 S. Main St., was once Calvert's original movie theater. It was built in 1929 and named after the owner Carl Allday's wife Eloise. It operated as the town movie house until 1960. During the Eloia's heyday, Miss Eloise sold tickets, while Carl and their son ran the projector and sold popcorn. It was pretty modern and upscale at the time, even featuring a cry room and double seats. After a fire ended its run, The Eloia sat empty and forlorn for decades. But now, it has been reinvented and is once again destined to be a great source of entertainment for the people of Calvert and surrounding Texas cities.

Entrepreneur Harold Maris was an antique dealer in the Houston area for 18 years. He bought the Eloia as a second location for his antique business. He painstakingly restored and renovated the building (doing much of the work with a paint roller himself). The unique setting of the historic theater makes antique shopping here a special treat.

But, Harold has since decided to utilize the historic building in ways that will further benefit the citizens of Calvert. The Eloia will now be a multifaceted facility, providing live music and theater entertainment and dining opportunities. The Sweet Shoppe, which is located in what was once the theater's lobby, features hand-dipped Bluebell Ice Cream, old-fashioned candies and homemade pies and pastries. And, Harold is currently turning the original balcony level into his apartment. What a great second life for this historical Calvert trademark. Watch the marquee for great things to come! Visit www.theeloia.com or call 979-364-3660.

TEXAS STAR FELINE PRESERVATION

Lions and Tigers and Bears . . . *oh no!* Your family is in for a truly memorable experience at the Texas Star Feline Preservation in Calvert, 5650 Springhill Rd. Owners and ranch staff are dedicated to the preservation of endangered animals. The park has lions, tigers, bears, longhorn cattle, paint horses, pumas, bobcats, monkeys, reptiles, wolves, birds, pigs and the park dogs "Zane and Tommie." The Texas Star Feline Preservation team work with many animal conservation and preservation groups to make sure these beautiful animals live on. The park is open to the public for private tours, over-night camping, birthday parties and picnics, and for learning experiences that will delight all ages. The property was once part of the famed Ellis Ranch and holds lots of history. There is also a 6,000-square-foot barn for private events and a 15-acre lake full of bass and catfish. Texas Feline Preservation is a must! Call 979-779-7230.

CALVERT HISTORICAL FOUNDATION

Established in 1968, Calvert Historical Foundation sponsors many educational events throughout the year that preserve and present the history of Robertson County in Calvert. Events like August Celebration where the town comes together with street dancing, live entertainment and an overall "celebration" of Calvert and its glorious past, is one of the projects they undertake each year.

The Foundation has also been instrumental in preserving many of the beautiful buildings and homes throughout the town. In fact, Calvert has an amazing 47 blocks of homes and businesses listed in the National Historic Register, the third largest historic district in Texas. By preserving information on historical sites, people, buildings and events, Calvert Historical Foundation has made a big impact in recording the wonderful history of Robertson County—and Texas—for future generations. For a schedule of activities, call 254-493-1327.

You will be delighted with your visit to this amazing little kolache shop, 709 Main St., in downtown Calvert. The story behind this success story is as sweet as the kolaches themselves. Owner Jody Powers, also known as "The Crazy Kolache Lady," has been featured on the *Texas Country Reporter* television show, in *Texas Highways* magazine, and the *Houston Chronicle.* She's wonderfully entertaining and has even been known to sing and towel dance in the street! But the star of this show is always her delicious kolaches. Jody spent many years learning to make kolaches using her grandmother Zamykal's recipe and says, "It's more than just a great recipe; it's learning to 'feel' the dough." Jody starts her 16-hour day at 12:30 am, baking all through the night, and now has 30 different kolaches—assorted fruits and nuts, yummy creams and savory meats. Jody is also in the process of expanding Zamykal Gourmet Kolaches into the building next door. (More sweet things to come!) Call 979-364-2386 or visit www.zamykalkolaches.com.

Bed & Breakfasts

Parish House Bed and Breakfast
A Step Back in Time

It's a house that you just hope is a bed and breakfast! With its cupola tower, decorative shingle work and gazebo porch, Parish House Bed and Breakfast, 609 E. Gregg St., is a historical treasure that exudes Victorian charm and elegance. Located in the center of Calvert's National Register Historic District, the B&B is one of only a few Queen Anne style houses of its kind remaining in the U.S. It was built in 1894 by Lee Henderson Parish, who acquired the plans for the house through a mail-order catalog. Owner Bronwyn McGlothlin has lovingly restored and renovated the beautiful home, furnishing it with incredible 19th century pieces. Guests rate their stay in this remarkable B&B as the "best they've ever experienced." Bronwyn loves that her guests feel at home in the Parish House and encourages them to enjoy it as their own. She is living her lifelong dream and loves sharing it with others. Call 979-574-5603 or visit www.parishbb.com.

"Cowboy Up" or rather "Dust yourself off when you fall, get back in the saddle, and keep on tryin'." Owners Sandra and David Hulsey of Cowboy Up Ranch Furniture have exemplified the true character and attitude of the American Cowboy and Cowgirl since 1997. Sandra, at an early age, learned this way of life from her father and grandfather, two true working cowboys. In fact, her grandfather was an honored Mounted Patrol Rider in Fort Worth.

And with just one visit to Cowboy Up, located at 404 S. Main St. in historic downtown Calvert, you're sure to join the Cowboy way of life, too. You will find everything to create your own cowboy palace.

"We pride ourselves in having a large selection of 'made in the USA' products," says Sandra. "And if you can imagine it…we can have it custom made for you, too."

Cowhides and cowhide-enhanced pieces, turquoise inlaid designs and intricate, hand-tooled leather goods, Cowboy Up's selection, from more than 400 supplies, will leave you breathless, and its prices will have you smiling all the way to check out (arms loaded, of course!). You'll choose from Cattleman's dining tables, buffalo hides, crocodile chairs and JJ Ranch antler chandeliers. You can even design a chandelier using your own antlers. The options are limitless! Popular lines include Cowboy Living, American West, 3D Leather Works, Naccona and Justin, just to name a few.

And the selection isn't the only thing that will leave you feeling warm and content. Once you hear the very first, 'Come right on in" and see the kind smiles of Cowboy Up's very knowledgeable and helpful staff, you'll feel right at home. Visit www.acowboyup.com or call 979-364-3744.

COUNTRY JAR MALL

Sometimes small towns hold the most incredible surprises. Calvert has quite a few of its own. The downtown historical district is a fantastic place to shop, and the locals are excited that their town is slowly gaining more recognition. Two people in Calvert who have worked hard to help the town move forward in attracting more retail and the arts are Randy and Jan Billingsly. They have opened Country Jar Mall, 702 Main St., a great space with an antique mall setting featuring various top-notch vendors. Browse through the vignettes for antiques, jewelry, collectibles and books, and you'll feel as though you've stepped back in time. The name was a clever combination of the first letters of their names—**J**an **A**nd **R**andy—Country JAR Mall. Look forward to great things happening here in this Calvert shopping venue. For more information or hours, call 254-493-1327.

Wooden Spoon

"Where everything stirred up is GREAT!"

Karol Allen believes, "When you have a passion for something, the love of that dream will become a reality with faith and hard work." Her dream-come-true is the Wooden Spoon, 726 S. Main St. She opened the original Calvert restaurant in another building in 2000 and with the motto, "Everything We Stir Up is Great," has built a reputation for amazing, fresh food using only the highest-quality ingredients. She purchased the current 134-year-old building, and with the help of many friends, renovated it from floor to ceiling into the colorful, fun space it is today—cool concrete floors, warm brick walls and lots of black and white check. The Wooden Spoon is open for lunch during the week and also for dinner during the weekend. You will love every single item on the menu, including Karol's specialty—homemade pies! Apple, peach, and blueberry fruit pies or lemon, chocolate, and banana cream pies are all favorites. Everything is homemade, and everything is delicious!! Call 979-364-2380.

BUTCH'S BRICK PIT BBQ

For more than 30 years, Butch Eustice has been in the auto painting business, but he always loved the art of "barbecue." In fact, he was winning BBQ cookoffs for 10 years when he and his wife Nelda finally decided that they were "smoking hot smokers." It was time to turn this favorite hobby into a business—a winning decision for them and the folks of Calvert. Butch's Brick Pit BBQ, 1621 S. Main St., features a large pit that is wrapped in specialized fire brick to maintain the heat. The 7-by-14 foot pit, which holds 100 briskets, can easily handle large catering demands and the large, 12-by-40 foot deck and inviting front porch with rockers allows them to host special events onsite. Try their delicious beef brisket, pork ribs, juicy chicken and turkey. You'll give it all a big blue ribbon! Call 979-364-0444.

Discover Salado

Salado is a perfect little hamlet of a village just a short drive from Austin, San Antonio or Dallas/Fort Worth. Sitting right in the heart of the beautiful wildflower country, and just minutes from two clear lakes, it offers visitors a peaceful respite and delightful retreat in the countryside, as well as superb shopping and entertainment opportunities. It's one of the first places we think of when it's time for a little "shopping therapy" for a fun ladies day out. It's a favorite "birthday trip," "romantic weekend" or exciting "holiday jumpstart." And it is recently gaining a reputation as a "wine town," which complements its longstanding reputation as an "Arts Community."

Wonderful little boutiques on Main Street—as well as the side streets—will keep you busy for a long weekend. So, the perfect way to enjoy Salado is to choose one of the incredible bed and breakfasts as home base, and take your time to explore and enjoy the town. Park your car at one end and make your way through each and every charming store. You'll find fine art, exquisite antiques and reproductions, handcrafted furniture, home décor, trendy fashions, gourmet food, wine and lovely, friendly people who will make you feel at home. The pace of this charming vintage village (population around 2000) is slow and easy-going, so join the locals in relishing each wonderful moment in Salado.

A Historic Treasure

Treasures abound in Salado, but the town itself is the greatest historic treasure. Its colorful history unfolds along the meandering spring-fed Salado Creek, which provided a cool oasis for the earliest Indians who lived here, the Spanish Explorers who first mapped the area and the veterans of the Texas Revolution who claimed land grants. Legend says that these early visitors believed that Salado Creek had special curative powers, and the town's sculpture "Sirena" is a tribute to the creek's spiritual tradition.

During the mid 1800s, progress rolled into the community with the coming of the Overland Stage and Pony Express Stop on the Old Chisholm Trail. The two area lakes and a river made it the perfect location for the stagecoach stop on the network of cattle trails from San Antonio. The historic **Stagecoach Inn**, 401 S. Stagecoach Rd., is the longest, continuous-running hotel in the state's history and during the early days was frequented by not only notable Texas dignitaries, but also a few notorious desperados.

Land for a village and a college was donated in 1859 by Col. E.S.C. Robertson, and the community of Salado was founded. People began to settle here to take advantage of the atmosphere the college created, and it was soon an agricultural center with its own gristmill. Salado was known as the "Athens of Texas." Salado College operated only until 1885, and then was the private Thomas Arnold High School from 1890-1913. (You'll read in this section about the beautiful **StoneCreek Settlement Bed and Breakfast**, which was built on a part of the historic Salado College site.)

When citizens began to move to the larger cities surrounding Salado, the population dropped to almost 400 by 1914, and then to almost 200 by 1950. Fortunately a revitalization began to take place in the small village soon after, inspired by the Central Texas Area Museum in 1959 and the new Mill Creek residential area and championship golf courses in 1960. In 1962, Grace Jones, a former New York model, purchased the old First State Bank building and opened an exclusive high-end fashion boutique. Clients were flown in by helicopter, and the trend for catering to the customers had begun. Shops and restaurants began to open to support the growth, and the popularity of the **Stagecoach Inn Restaurant** continued to draw visitors to Salado. Today, more than 130 wonderful businesses add a unique charm to the village, making it a destination for great shopping and fun.

Small Town Paradise

More than 140 years after Salado's beginning, its historical pride, friendly spirit and genuine hospitality are still evident throughout the community. You'll be greeted by warm smiles and friendly waves everywhere you go, and find it to be one of the most enchanting and beautiful places anywhere in Texas. The shopping is incredible; art lovers consider it their home away from home; outstanding bed and breakfasts are ready to wow; and the village hosts wonderful special events throughout the year.

Salado Village has been described as being, "the best art town in Texas," offering visitors fine selections of fine art, art gallery tours, and instruction in a variety of art media. Your group would love visiting during one of the many art fairs in the village or meeting one of the talented artist as they create in their studios and galleries.

Every shop you enter will become your "most favorite." Feather your nest with treasures from long-loved shops like **Charlotte's of Salado**, **Christy's**, **Splendors of Salado** and **Side by Side**. These beautiful stores hold the most unique home décor, luxurious linens, popular kitchen gadgets, wonderful jewelry, and fun fashions. Or, discover a "fountain of youth" in the selection of cutting-edge skin care and cosmetics at **The Apothecary** on Main Street.

You'll need sustenance to keep going, and Salado will surely satisfy. You would imagine that such a perfect little shopping village has at least one charming tearoom. It does! In fact, there are several wonderful places that offer the perfect pause during a fun-filled shopping day.

Salado is also becoming a destination for folks who like to "swirl, sniff and sip" the fruit of the vine. The **Salado Creek Winery & Vineyard** and **The Vineyard at Florence** offer visitors beautiful venues for wine tastings, wine tours, musical entertainment and special events, and are on the annual San Gabriel Wine Tour each June.

Finally, at the end of a wonderful day of treasure hunting, glassblowing, history tours or even skydiving, let the charm of one of the remarkable Salado bed and breakfasts wrap you in their beauty and comfort. From historic homes and country houses to a "settlement" of restored cottages, you'll find a wonderful place to stay.

We know you will absolutely fall in love with Salado. The innkeepers, artists, merchants, restaurateurs and wine-makers have worked together to create on of the most beautiful and charming communities in Texas. It's sure to become your favorite place for a "Ladies Day Out!"

For more information, call the Village of Salado Tourism Office at 254-947-8634 or visit www.saladotx.gov, or call the Salado Chamber of Commerce at 254-947-5040 or visit www.salado.com.

Salado
Fairs Festivals & Fun

February
Taste of Salado

March
Wildflower Art Show

July
Salado Legends at Tablerock
Silver Spur Theatre Original Melodrama

August
Salado Legends at Tablerock
Silver Spur Theatre Original Melodrama

September
Chocolate and Wine Weekend

October
Chirstmas in October
Annual Art Fair
Tablerock's Fright Trail

November
Annual Gathering of the Scottish Clans

December
Salado's Christmas Stroll
Tablerock's "A Christmas Carol"
Silver Spur Theatre Christmas "On the Air"

Artists & Art Galleries

GRIFFITH FINE ART GALLERY

More than 15 artists are showcased in this beautiful Salado art gallery. Works include landscapes, Western art, wildlife, still lifes, pottery, sculpture, stained glass, commissioned portraits, and an impressive collection of abstracts. Griffith Fine Art Gallery is located at 229 N. Main St.—a collector's delight. This gallery carries original oils, acrylics, watercolors, pastels, bronzes and custom jewelry. Owner and abstract artist, Kay Griffith, is committed to developing the gallery, as well as education in the arts. During the Salado Christmas Stroll, the gallery is open late, so visitors can shop for unique and beautiful pieces of art. Call 254-947-3177 or to see the featured artists, visit www.griffithfineartgallery.com.

SALADO ARTS WORKSHOP

What started with a passion for glass art on a weekend whim has grown (with the support and encouragement of Salado) into a remarkable organization dedicated to helping others learn and benefit from the art of glassmaking. A group of talented, professional artists provides demonstrations and classes for both students and adults, and parties can be scheduled. Learn to blow a delicate glass Easter egg, a glass flower or even a beautiful Christmas ornament at Salado Arts Workshop, 113 Salado Plaza Dr. Classes are offered in glassblowing, stained glass, glass etching and glass fusing, as well as drawing, painting, soap making, sculpture and more. Glass artist Andrea McLester is a studio jeweler whose clientele includes some of the world's leading dance and opera companies, with designs featured in several books. With a belief that "Art Changes Lives," the workshop also makes and provides beautiful "glass hands" for children in crisis, in select hospitals. Call 254-654-9171 or visit www.saladoartsworkshop.org.

Attractions & Entertainment

It's described as "historically funny" and a "house of laughter." Grab the family and head for the Salado Silver Spur Theater for a memorable night of Vaudeville, classic cinema or live musical entertainment. The theater is located at 108 Royal St. within the historic Guest and Sanford Granary, a group of 1950s buildings that have been converted into a 150-seat theater. It's the only one-of-its-kind in Texas. Owner Grainger Esch once performed as a clown for the Ringling Bros. Barnum & Bailey Circus and has worked in television and movies. He and the entire cast of professional performers are passionate about "laughter" and dedicated to spreading it. You might see a stage play, a silent movie with musical accompaniment or a live variety show. The performers are in perpetual motion, using slapstick and satire, pratfalls and pranks and music and magic to keep you thoroughly entertained. The space is also available for private events. In fact, you might have seen it in the news a few years ago as the venue for Jenna Bush's bridal dinner. Visit www.saladosilverspur.com or call 254- 947-3456.

StoneCreek Settlement
Bed & Breakfast

Jill and Johnny Shipman moved to Salado to retire, but with their creative energy and natural gift for hospitality, they realized that this was just a new beginning. In no time they found a beautiful piece of land and began construction on Stonecreek Settlement Bed & Breakfast, 714 College Hill. Using reclaimed wood from early Texas homes and historic buildings, they built each of the seven cottages to reflect the style of the early Texas and German Sunday House cottages that were once so prevalent in the Hill Country. With gracious gardens, antique architectural elements and beautiful furnishings, the guest cottages are unparalleled in their charm. The Shipmans say, "We wanted to create a place reminiscent of days gone by when folks lived in small settlements and had time to sit out on the front porch."

The rooms feature limestone fireplace mantels, stained glass, punched tin window valances and pine flooring, but have modern amenities including Jacuzzi tubs. Wonderful! Visit www.stonecreeksettlement.com or call 254-947-9099. *(See related story on page 236.)*

The gracious hospitality and intimate seclusion of this Salado getaway will wrap you in charm and romance and make your visit truly unforgettable. Inn on the Creek, 602 Center Cir., is an elegant 14-room Victorian Inn nestled alongside the peaceful Salado Creek. Owners Will Lowery and Chris Spradley combine their creative energy and gifts for hospitality in this premier bed and breakfast. They love introducing their guests to the rich culture of the Village of Salado.

All of the buildings on the property were built in the late 1800s and moved to their present location in 1987. Will and Chris have renovated the three-story Victorian Manor into private guest rooms that are filled with American and English antiques and luxurious modern amenities. Inn on the Creek has the reputation for offering private club-style service and gourmet, 5-star dining. A four-course dining experience is offered each Friday and Saturday evening. Cocktails are served on the porches overlooking the beautiful creek, and dinner is served in one of four first-floor dining rooms. Can you imagine anything more romantic? There is also an intimate bar called Alexander's Distillery on the second- and third-floors where you can enjoy drinks and entrees.

Plan a picnic alongside the creek banks; cozy up in one of the hammocks with a good book and a glass of wine or stroll through the charming Village shops just a few blocks away. And, at the end of a wonderful day, snuggle into luxurious bedding by Compfy. You will love it so much you'll be thankful that you can purchase a set of sheets to take home. Inn on the Creek is pure luxury, beauty, charm and romance. It is sure to become your favorite place for a wonderful, intimate weekend getaway. Call 254-947-5554, 877-947-5554 or visit www.inncreek.com. *(See related story on page 234.)* *(Color photo featured in front section of the book.)*

Baines House

Bed, Breakfast & Beyond Inn
Salado, Texas

Merging Texas history with special comforts and wonderful luxuries, Rod and Sheryl Russell invite you to be their guest in a beautiful place that "feels like someone's just pressed the world's pause button." Baines House Bed, Breakfast & Beyond Inn, 316 Royal St., is a collection of quaint cottages and a beautiful main house that was once the home of Rev. George Washington Baines, the great grandfather of President Lyndon Baines Johnson. The original Greek Revival, Texas "dogtrot-style" house now recorded as a Texas and National Historic Landmark was the Russells' home for eight years before they renovated and moved into an old barn that connects to the property by way of a wooden bridge.

When the Russells relocated from the Dallas area to Salado and into the Baines House, they had no intention of turning it into a bed and breakfast. However, friends would visit and stay in the guesthouse. Soon others were calling to see if they could rent it for the weekend. With their outgoing personalities, love for entertaining, artistic talents and great culinary skills, the Russells were natural born innkeepers. They have since expanded the bed and breakfast into nine lodgings that include cottages, suites and cozy havens. King-size beds, private baths, bar areas and tranquil gardens grace each one. One room has a sunken, outdoor tub surrounded by stained glass and lattice, and five have jetted tubs. Art and antiques are combined with faux finishes and designer inspiration throughout the inn, but the food is one of the main attractions. (Sheryl is the artist, and Rod is the cook!) Incredible breakfasts are served each morning in the Carriage House, and a yummy dessert is always on the menu. (The Russells believe in eating dessert as soon as possible each day—and that includes breakfast!). You'll love their "sweet" philosophy of life and genuine Southern hospitality. Call 254-947-5260, 866-725-2367 or visit www.baineshouse.com.

Red Barn Hideaway

It's close to everything, but away from it all! Red Barn Hideaway, 231 College Hill Dr., is just a short walk from all of Salado's great shopping, but you may not want to venture out once you've checked in to this Oasis! Owners Debbie and Ron Harrison describe their cozy bed-and-breakfast as "Salado country style, with aged wood and antiques—a pleasing, comfortable space that wraps its arms around you." Enjoy the views of wildlife from the outside deck and a delicious breakfast each morning. Hideaway Cottage is a two bedroom, one bath with a full kitchen that is available for larger groups. Call 254-947-1974 or visit www.redbarnhideaway.com.

Fun fashions for all ages, beautiful jewelry, wonderful accessories, all in one fabulous boutique! Christy's of Salado, #5 Salado Sq. (tucked behind Side by Side and Magnolia's) has been a favorite destination for 18 years. Owner Christy Goodfellow says, "We have a wonderfully loyal customer base ranging in age from youthful 20s to vibrant 90s from all over the US." And, she loves dressing them all! Christy opened the doors to her shop right out of college at the young age of 23, and has grown it through the years into a premier ladies' boutique specializing in "casual clothes you love to live in!" Design apparel includes Barbara Lesser, Kathleen Sommers, Tianello and Johnny Was. We loved her great line of shoes (among others) called Volatile Footware, and the designer jewelry from Treska and Ayala Bar. Christy also specializes in easy-care wigs for fashion or for need. Call 254-947-0561.

You'll be surprised and delighted when you walk through the Texas-style door of The Howling Wolff, 560 N. Main St. Half of this shop is a fashion boutique and the other filled with furniture and home décor. While vacationing (and shopping) in New Mexico, mother and daughter-in-law, Liz and Krystal Wolff were inspired to bring the wonderful Southwestern clothing and accessories they loved to Salado. Krystal oversees the boutique's great women's clothing, boots, jewelry and accessories with a modern Western twist from well-known designers like Double D Ranch, Young Essence, Cowgirl Tuff Company, Old Gringo Boots, GypsySoule and B.B. Simon. From bright, colorful dresses, gauzy shirts and flattering jeans to soft leather jackets, appliquéd "cowgirl" boots and unusual jewelry, you'll love the trendy, Southwestern fashions. Pair a short, colorful, sassy dress with flower motif, Western boots and fabulous silver jewelry, or find cool, casual items perfect for our Texas climate and easy lifestyle. Visit www.thehowlingwolff.com or call 254-947-0600. *(See related story on page 230 .)*

Side by Side
artful expressions for you and your home

Julie Lowe felt like she was doing what God intended her to do when she opened her first store Splendors of Salado. She combined her love of decorating with her business degree and years of personnel and sales experience. With that a success, Julie opened a sister store, Side by Side, at #21 N. Main St. Here you'll find the same elegant style in furniture and home décor—just more WOW! Eclectic furniture and home accessories include wall-size mirrors and fireplace mantels, large decorative urns, metal sculptures, beautiful wool rugs and filigree birdcages. You'll also love the great selection of fun and ever-popular Yellow Box Shoes, and colorful, chunky jewelry and unique purses. The store is clean and sleek, with buttery hardwood floors and cool colored walls, and so much fun to shop. Call 254-947-7220 or visit www.saladosidebyside.com. *(See related story page 233.)*

Walk through the bright red door of this beautiful store into a world of elegance and Old World charm. Charlotte's of Salado, #8 Rock Creek Dr., has long been a favorite place to shop for incredible home décor and accessories. Owner Charlotte Douglass wants you to, "Indulge yourself, your home…or someone special!" Her creativity is evident throughout every room in the store, and the shopping experience all starts with a warm cup of gourmet coffee. "It's just Southern hospitality!" she says. Enjoy a cup of the popular Seasons of Salado blend and take your time browsing through her remarkable selection of fine furnishings and gifts.

Charlotte has a Master's degree in counseling but a passion for interior design. "I use my degree every day," she says, "I really listen to the needs of my customers, and I respect their pocketbooks. I never carry anything I would not buy myself, and I shop hard to find beauty and value."

Her strength also lies creating beautiful spaces with ordinary things. For instance, we bought a beautiful Pashmina scarf right off the table, where it was being used as a table runner! She uses unusual accent pieces, fabulous throw pillows and wonderful wall hangings to create a style that mixes Tuscan romance, Shabby Chic and Old World elegance.

Charlotte has always been an integral part of the Salado community, and in fact, was the village's first elected mayor. She is also a breast cancer survivor, happy to be well and able to do what she truly loves—helping customers make their homes a beautiful

reflection of who they are. Her spectacular displays are always changing, always stunning and always current. "Indulge yourself, your home…or someone special!" Visit www.charlottesofsalado.com or call 254-947-0240.

Sofi's
At the Stagecoach

Ingamaj (Ing) Knutsson has lived and worked in many countries around the world. She has always been fascinated by various cultures and their stunning folk art. When she moved to Salado in 1998, she decided to introduce her love of folk art to the area. She opened INGS, an eclectic store with inventory from as far away as Africa and Indonesia. In 2006, she expanded on her idea and opened SOFI'S at the Stagecoach; 401 S. Main St. Ing invited several other like-minded, small storeowners to join her. The result? A wonderfully fascinating store, that offers African, Asian and South American folkart, wearable art, Flax and so much more. Sofi's also

specializes in nativities from around the world. There's even a store mascot—an adorable Schnauzer named Flicka! So much to see and so much fun to be had! For more information, visit www.sofissalado.com or call 254-947-4336.

Mother and daughter-in-law, Liz and Krystal Wolff, have one of the most fun and exciting shops in Salado. Half of The Howling Wolff, 560 N. Main St., is filled with great Southwestern fashion, and the rest is a collection of exciting, colorful and very unusual furniture and home décor. While vacationing in New Mexico, the two were inspired to open this unique store, which will make you think you are shopping the quaint streets of Santa Fe. Liz fills this part of the store with wonderful items like turquoise painted furniture, cowhide rugs and rustic iron accessories. Brightly colored and tooled headboards, leather throw pillows, feathered floral arrangements and stunning mirrors and lamps all have a colorful Southwest flair, and the accessories fit beautifully into any décor. Just one of their soft throws or decorative pillows can add the colors of the New Mexico sunset to an ordinary room. Look fabulous and live well with something wonderful from The Howling Wolff. Call 254-947-0600 or visit www.thehowlingwolff.com. *(See related story page 227.)*

When Jill Bookout turned 47 she turned her life in a completely new direction when she decided to follow her heart and make a life-long dream come true. She took a leap of faith and opened Taylors, 600 N. Main St., a wonderful and very successful home décor and specialty shop in Salado's charming shopping district. The center itself was built to resemble an "old-timey" town. Step inside to casual elegance from the rustic exterior and you'll find everything from beautiful furniture and accessories to fancy jewels. Sumptuous pillows, exotic florals, tabletop décor, mirrors and more are beautifully displayed to help customers envision them in their own homes. It's a reflection of Jill's passion. "I love meeting people and helping them create a comfortable and beautiful space they call 'home,'" she says. "So many of my customers have become like family."

Family has always been important to Jill. In fact, the store is named for her sweet grandmother who always encouraged her creativity. She says, "Even as a little girl I loved looking at all of her beautiful crystal, china and silver, and loved its delicate elegance. I was so touched that she left all of it to me when she passed away. She has been my inspiration through this exciting adventure in my life."

You will love browsing through this enchanting space filled with special things. From have-to-have candlesticks and delicious candles to beautiful table runners and unique serving pieces, you are sure to find a treasure for your home or for someone you love. And, you are sure to make a new friend in Jill. Call 254-947-8084.

AT SALADO

The Apothecary at Salado, located at 418 N. Main St. in the heart of historic Salado, offers organic cosmetic, skincare, bath and body, and lifestyle products in an elegant art gallery setting. In addition to the quality products that it carries, The Apothecary showcases work from Texas artists like Bill Reily, Michael Frary, Edmund Kinzinger, and sculptor Jesus Moroles.

Owner Gayle Sullivan has created this beautiful boutique that she hopes "transports you to a place where your spirit is revitalized through a unique combination of sight, sound and smell." Gayle provides makeup sessions for brides, bridal parties and special occasions. She personalizes each customer's session, using only the highest quality products by Zuii and Nouba. These lines are especially popular with groups of all ages and those who must avoid chemicals for medical reasons. The Apothecary recently added new organic bath and bodylines—Patyka from Paris, Kai from Malibu, and Niven Morgan from Dallas. It also

offers bamboo linens and clothing from Nandina Future Fibers and Yala, and unique jewelry by Stacey Shade and Arabella Dalton. And, if you're looking for a new fragrance, you'll love the selection by Carthusia from the Isle of Capri; Estaban, blended jointly by perfumers in Paris and Japan; and Profumi Del Forte from Tuscany. Rigaud candles from Paris, the original fragrance candles burned exclusively in the White House by Jacqueline Kennedy and favored by Frank Sinatra, transports customers to a nostalgic place and time.

Visit www.theapothecaryatsalado.com for Twitter and Facebook links or call 254-947-7273.

We love, love, love this adorable kitchen and gift boutique. Splendors of Salado, #4 Rock Creek Dr., is located within a wonderful old house off Main Street, and is just a joy to shop. Owner Julie Lowe is a sweet soul who combines her love of people, her business experience and her passion for decorating and staging homes in this wonderful store. The shop's kitchen has a corner sink that looks out over a creek, and the kitchen is filled with, of course, everything for the kitchen (including the kitchen sink!) Specialty kitchen items include beautiful linens by April Cornell and others, cooking tools and gadgets you never knew you had to have, pottery, bar accessories, napkins and cookbooks. In one room, there is also a children's boutique called, "For This Child," filled with wonderful children's clothing, books, toys and treasures. And, be sure to wander outside to see the yard full of garden items. "Splendid" selections of beautiful things! Call 254-947-3630 or visit www.splendorsofsalado.com.

(See related story on page 228.)

Ambrosia Tea Room

"Come back to a time when there was rest for the spirit and sweetness for the soul." Jenny Moore's motto for her charming Salado Tearoom perfectly describes her desire to nourish her customers with delicious food and sweet, Southern hospitality. Ambrosia Tea Room, 102 N. Main St., is a favorite place for friends to gather for luncheons, showers, Sunday afternoon celebrations and fun English teas. The atmosphere is feminine and fun—black and white rooms decorated with vintage clothing, hats and jewelry, and antique furniture displaying books, candles and tea-related gift items. From yummy homemade soups (the selection changes daily) to old-fashioned finger sandwiches and Ambrosia's famous Chicken Avocado Salad, everything is wonderful! Jenny attributes Ambrosia Tea Room's continued success to the former owner, sweet Mrs. Jane, who taught her everything she knows. Call 254-947-3733.

Alexander's Distillery

Inn on the Creek, 602 Center Cir., is one of the most charming and luxurious inns you will ever visit. The historic manor is located along the banks of Salado Creek where guests can enjoy all that Salado has to offer while being pampered with true Southern hospitality. It is also home to Alexander's Distillery, a handsome, upscale restaurant and bar located on the second floor of the inn. The restaurant was named after the distillery that was located on the grounds from 1861-1865. It apparently aided in the "Civil War efforts" by providing soldiers with liquor for both "opiate and stimulate" services! Inn and restaurant owners Will Lowery and Chris Spradley have created a sophisticated space filled with wonderful, original artwork. With stunning views of Salado Creek, it's the perfect place to enjoy an evening of drinks and great food. Call 254-947-5554, 877-947-5554 or visit www.inncreek.com. *(See related story on page 224.)*

The exterior of this charming Salado bistro resembles a quaint seaside resort—complete with an all white porch and comfy rocking chairs. The food, however, is "grandma's with a flair." Sisters Jennifer Lohse Angell and Lea Anne Lohse Erwin hatched the idea for Adelea's as little girls, when they used to record episodes of Julia Child's cooking show and try to copy the menu. Even though their grandmother Adele passed away before they were born, their mother used her recipes to revel the girls with stories of her life. The sisters created Adelea's, 302 N. Main St., as a tribute to their grandmother's memory. Both Jennifer and Lea Anne left the corporate world in 2005 to start Adelea's Catering, while they both studied at the Texas Culinary Academy in Austin. When Lea Anne decided to follow her husband to law school, she sold her half to Jennifer's husband Kelly, who now works as the head chef. Adelea's also hosts a weekly, Saturday morning Farmer's Market throughout the summer and is available for special events. Adelea's has also become a favorite venue for rehearsal dinners, showers, children's birthdays and English teas. For information call 254-947-0018 or visit www.adeleas.com.

Old Salado Bakery

Facing I-35 at Exit 284 (100 N. Church St.), this family-owned bakery and coffee shop caters both to first-time traveling visitors and long-time Salado natives as a comfy spot to stop for good food and refreshment. The building is an old farmhouse built in 1930 that was abandoned until 2006, when it was restored as a bakery by Roy Tyson. It is now managed by John Davis. Roy T's is famous for melt-in-your-mouth Southern Maid doughnuts, New Orleans beignets and fruit Kolaches. They sell the finest Community Coffee, Dublin Dr. Pepper, homemade soups, salads, pizzas, cakes and pies. You can also get a strong espresso. The café has become such a local favorite that you'll often find it crowded with other artists, musicians and business folks from Salado. It's a family and pet friendly place—definitely more than just a coffee stop along the highway. Call 254-947-7181 or visit www.oldsaladobakery.com.

StoneCreek Settlement
Special Event Venue

Jill and Johnny Shipman fell in love with Salado after their very first visit. They realized it was the perfect place to retire. Of course, typical retirement was not an option for this creative couple. They decided to build the StoneCreek Settlement Bed & Breakfast complex, 714 College Hill. Visitors enjoy luxurious lodging in seven private cottages and have access to the Settlement House and the lush grounds for weddings, corporate events and special celebrations. From the moment he asks, "Will you?" to the day you say, "I do," the Shipmans will help customize a spectacular wedding on their beautiful property. From a gorgeous garden ceremony to a lavish dinner reception, StoneCreek Settlement has everything you need to make your special day a memorable success. Call 254-947-9099 or visit www.stonecreeksettlement.com. *(See related story on page 223.)*

Wines & Wineries

Gather with friends to swirl and sip delicious wines, enjoy appetizers and listen to great Texas music. Salado Creek Winery & Vineyard, 227 N. Main St., is a family-owned winery that, along with many international awards, has won the heart of its community. Owners Jon and Dottie Moore had been making wine for many years (Jon since the age of 16!) before turning their passion into a business. When tropical storm Hermine washed all their inventory and winemaking equipment downstream, many Salado business owners pitched in to help them recover and reopen the winery. Today Salado Creek produces the only award-winning wines from Bell County and has captured the 2011 Grand Star award from the Lonestar International Wine Competition for its Salado Frost Icewine! It also makes a series of citrus wines, which include a Texas lemon wine made from Rio Grande Valley fruit—one of our favorites! The tasting room is open daily, and tasting classes are available for groups of eight or more. Meet the family at www.saladoswirlandsip.com or call 254-947-9000. Live music on weekends March-December.

THE VINEYARD
AT FLORENCE

Breathtaking vineyard vistas, gentle Hill Country breezes, wine tastings, polo match-es, tranquil spa services and magnificent outdoor spaces for special events; The Vineyard at Florence has something for everyone. Even though it will seem as though you are on a Tuscany hillside, The Vineyard is located north of Austin less than 20 minutes outside of Salado at 8711 W FM 487. It is a desired destination for weddings and corporate events and a favorite place for group culinary classes or day and weekend seminars and retreats. Enjoy a glass of hand-crafted, award-winning wine at the Italian-inspired tasting villa

overlooking the 30-acre vineyard and be sure to check out scheduled wine trails and tastings. The Vine-yard is a wonderful place to gather with friends for a memorable eve-ning, and an incredible venue for a romantic "Florence" wedding. Visit www.thevineyardatflorence.com or call 254-793-3363.

Texas Hill Country

Goldthwaite

San Saba

Lampasas

Discover Goldthwaite

Ask a few Goldthwaite natives what it was like to grow up here, and the answers are usually pretty similar. "It was like growing up in Mayberry, USA." Folks sat out on their porches until dark, sipping lemonade, and everyone knew everyone. Children played outside till they were called in at suppertime, and if they had been in any kind of mischief that day, someone in town knew about it (and would tell). It's still that kind of town. The folks are friendly and community-minded; they still tip their hats and wave (even to strangers), and they love to celebrate little events in a big way. They are also proud that Goldthwaite is known as the "Entrance to the Texas Hill Country." The land is pretty—beautiful rolling hills, pasturelands and native trees that attract hunters from across the country for deer, quail, dove and turkey. And, with 135 miles of rivers and streams, it's also a fisherman's paradise.

Past and Present Goldthwaite

Goldthwaite was established in 1885, with the coming of the Gulf, Colorado and Santa Fe Railways, and was named for Joe G. Goldthwaite, the railroad official who conducted the auction of town lots. It was part of Brown County until Mills County was organized in 1887, and was then named the county seat. The original Mills County Courthouse was built in 1890, burned in 1912, and rebuilt the following year.

In Goldthwaite, a visit to the Chamber of Commerce could land you in jail! The Chamber is located at 1001 E. Fisher St, (inside the historic jailhouse). If walls could talk, the original Mills County Jailhouse might have quite a few interesting stories about the wild, frontier days of Goldthwaite.

Although this part of the country was off the route of the Spanish explorations, it is recorded that Pedro Vial passed through the area between 1786 and 1789 while exploring a route from San Antonio to Santa Fe. The region was a hunting ground for the Comanche and Apache Indians who warred constantly for the land. During the Civil War and for decades after, settlers fought not only hostile Indians but also cattle rustlers, horse thieves and army deserters. The territory was nearly lawless during the early 1880s, and the early pioneers lived through almost three decades of frightening Indian raids. There was no court, no jail and almost no law enforcement, so the need for a jailhouse was obvious. The limestone jailhouse, Mills County's first government structure, was completed in 1888. At that time, the sheriff and his family lived on the first floor, and the prisoners were kept upstairs. (And, of course, the sheriff's wife was expected to do the cooking!) The cellblock walls are still etched with names and dates of prisoners who would sometimes keep calendars of their days behind bars.

Bridges to the Past

Spanning the 340-foot width of the Colorado River and connecting Mills and San Saba Counties, is one of the last three remaining suspension bridges still open to traffic in Texas. **The Regency Suspension Bridge**, built in 1939, replaced the original bridge built in 1903 and was restored and rededicated in 1999. The bridge that was built primarily by hand and with hand tools, is supported by permanent abutment towers set upon concrete foundations in the Colorado River. Flooring for the bridge consists of 4' x 12' planks nailed into place. It is reported that, during the construction of the famous bridge, workers had to be suspended in the air as they installed each of the support cables. It is really an amazing structure, and has been placed on the National Register of Historic Places.

Still want more history? The majority of Mills County and Goldthwaite history can be found in the **Mills County Historical Museum,** 1119 Fisher St., with artifacts and exhibits that date back to the earliest days. There is a Native American exhibit that includes primitive carvings and stone tools, items from the original train depot, military items from both World Wars, printing equipment from the original *Goldthwaite Eagle* and historical records available for genealogy research. Plan a long visit in the museum because there is so much to see!

Goldthwaite is extremely excited about its new museum on Legacy Plaza called **Texas Botanical Gardens & Native American Interpretation Center.** Here, visitors can "leap" thousands of years back in Mills County and Texas history through interactive exhibits and hands-on learning opportunities.

Charms of Goldthwaite

The past is always fascinating, but this charming Hill Country community celebrates the present in every possible way. There are festivals and parties throughout the year that draw visitors from across Texas, and one of the town's favorites is the **Mills County BBQ & Goat Cook-Off.** Yep, it's a goat cook-off! Proclaimed by the Governor as the official State Championship BBQ & Goat Cook-Off—enthusiastic winners become eligible to advance to the National Competition. Held in the city park under the large shade trees, folks gather to choose the best "cabrito" cooked in the county. There is a dance, arts and crafts fair, live music, car show, lots of food, of course, and even a "best dressed goat" contest. Throughout the year, there are rodeos, trail drives, quilt shows and car shows, but the city really comes to life during the holidays. Goldthwaite is on the Texas Hill Country Regional Christmas Lighting Trail, providing a magical experience of spectacular lighting and splendid shopping during the holiday season.

Goldthwaite is such a friendly, laidback town with a pride in its history and its people. Just ask them about one of their most famous citizens, **Jody Conradt**. She played basketball for Goldthwaite High School, and then for Baylor University, then coached at Waco Midway High School. She went on to be the head coach for the women's team at the University of Texas at Austin, with a coaching career that spanned 38 years. By retirement, Coach Conradt had tallied 900 career victories, second in all time victories for a NCAA Division I college basketball coach.

Saving the Best for Last

Small towns are usually filled with great little boutiques and charming stores, and Goldthwaite is no exception. From great Western furniture and gourmet foods to clothing, jewelry and unique home décor, you're sure to find something wonderful. And, at the end of the day, enjoy a night at the **Fisher Street Bed and Breakfast** or the beauty of the Hill Country at the **Rafter B Ranch**. Mills County is also known for its many pecan groves and is home to the "King and Queen of Pecans, DeWayne and Patty McCasland. Read their fascinating story (Page), then visit **Pecans.com** in the original Southern Pacific Railroad siding. We think you'll agree that a day in Goldthwaite is All That and Then Some!

For additional information on Goldthwaite, call Mills County Chamber of Commerce at 325-648-3619 or visit www.goldthwaite.biz.

Goldthwaite
Fairs Festivals & Fun

April
> Annual State Championship BBQ & Goat Cook-off
> Annual Easter Egg Hunt

May
> Car Show

June
> Farmers Market

July
> Farmers Market
> Independence Day Celebration

August
> Farmers Market

October
> Annual Quilt Show

November
> Hunter's Appreciation Wild Game Supper

December
> Annual Parade of Lights and Santa

Bed and Breakfasts, Cottages & Inns

Rafter B Ranch House

Located atop a scenic hill at 221 FM 574 W., the Rafter B Ranch House offers guests the pleasure of complete seclusion and privacy just two miles from Goldthwaite. The house was built in 1941 by Earl Tanner Fairman for use as a hunting lodge and constructed of materials from an old mill on the historic Williams Ranch. There is also a saloon bar from Mexico, and a 1920s bank vault door from the Star State Bank!

When Joe and Gail Brooks and Keith and Brenda Brooks bought the 307 acres in 2003, which includes the Rafter B Ranch House, they initially intended it to be a weekend getaway for family members. Never did they dream how many reunions, weddings, retreats, meetings and parties would take place in this beautiful place. The 5,000-square-foot ranch house includes five bedrooms, four baths and sleeps 18 comfortably. There are also three-camper hookups onsite. Call 432-639-2992 or visit www.rafterbranchhouse.com.

Fisher Street
Bed & Breakfast

Goldthwaite is a charming little town of about 2,000 nestled in the beautiful Hill Country of Central Texas. Besides the historical charm and friendly hospitality of its locals, the town is also known for its large herds of mohair goats, splendid shopping and great whitetail deer, quail and dove hunting. For a weekend in this charming town to explore the countryside, or do a little shopping, we've found the most wonderful place full of warmth and cozy hospitality. A visit to Fisher Street Bed & Breakfast, 1402 Fisher St., feels like "coming home to grandma's house." Warm wooden floors, arched doorways, large windows, French doors that open from one room to the other, and furnishings that invite hours of comfort and offer guests the perfect place to rest while exploring the beautiful area.

Owner Suzanne Doggett's bed and breakfast has been furnished and accessorized with her mother's furniture and dishes. Her gift for hospitality is evident by the care she puts into the homemade breads, muffins and fresh-made jam for breakfast. Suzanne says, "My mother and grandmother loved to cook and entertain. We always had teas and Sunday brunches and Christmas Open Houses for family and friends. I am so glad that I can continue that tradition for my guests."

The old-fashioned cottage style home features two bedrooms with queen-size beds and two baths, and a smaller bedroom with a day bed. There is a common living room, dining room and sunroom—perfect for reading the morning paper. If you are lucky enough to visit during the holidays, you will enjoy lighting displays, a Parade of Lights and festive  holiday fare in all of the town's specialty shops. Call 325-938-5247, 325-938-6619 or visit www.fisherstreetbedandbreakfast.com.

GW Upholstery – Rafter W Furniture

Whether you live on a ranch or in the big city, custom upholstered furniture in luxurious leathers, fabrics or textures can make your home a showplace. Picture antique Victorian settees in leopard-suede velvet, studded leather wingbacks atop zebra rugs and sofas covered in a combination of hair-on-hide and smooth leathers. You will love the unique collection of fine custom furniture and upholstered pieces at G W Upholstery and Rafter W Furniture.

Owner Gary Warlick learned the art of upholstery in 1972 and began upholstering fulltime in 1990. At that time, he and wife Carole purchased the historic building at 1014 4th St. on Goldthwaite's downtown square, which locals remember through the years as a doctor's office, pharmacy and gift shop. Gary and Carole say that many customers come in and recall having had a soda at the beautiful old marble bar, which they have kept in the showroom. Now displayed throughout the space are Gary's high-quality custom leather pieces and unique furniture. Gary's specialty is redesigning furniture and accessories with beautiful fabrics or leather and high-quality workmanship that can be used to decorate the most elegant of homes. Gary and Carole work with many suppliers of fine furniture, leathers and fabrics and can produce unique pieces and styles, ranging from sleek contemporary to ornate Mexican Colonial. Whether you bring in one of your special pieces to be reupholstered or purchase something Gary has already completed—it will be a treasure.

"There is no assembly line," says Gary. "I personally detail each piece of furniture to ensure quality workmanship. We can help showcase your special pieces or just 'cowboy-up' your ranch." His reputation for quality and attention to detail has spread throughout Texas, and some of his work has been included in the coffee table book, *Lone Star Living: Texas Homes and Ranches* by Tyler Beard. Call 325-648-2415 or visit www.rafterwfurniture.com.

McMahan Pharmacy Services, Inc.

Mike McMahan's mission is to deliver the highest quality pharmaceutical care to his customers, which is exactly what he has done since 1975. The staff at McMahan Pharmacy Services, Inc., 1503 W. Front St., believes in a holistic approach to healthcare and wellness. They offer natural medicines, vitamins, and herbs, in addition to traditional drug therapies. They even carry their own line of professionally formulated products and offer medication compounding. Mike has been a pillar of Goldthwaite and is known and appreciated by the community. Visit the RX Wellness Center at McMahan Pharmacy to learn more about natural medicines and nutrition or to pick up a greeting card for a friend. Visit www.mcmahanpharmacy.com or call 325-648-2484.

Live Oak Florist & Garden Center

Gina Love's life and career have come full circle. As owner of Live Oak Florist & Garden Center, Gina never imagined that the passion for flowers she discovered at such a young age would be a driving force in her life. Gina and her family moved to Goldthwaite in 1973 and when her father passed away a few months later, a wonderful couple named Estelle and Glen Dewitt adopted her mother and her as lifelong friends. Because they owned the garden center where Gina's mother worked, Gina grew up learning about flowers. It was only natural when she later opened her own garden center "with just ten flats of flowers on saw horses in front of her husband's office building." That colorful collection grew into three garden houses, three shade areas and a beautiful garden and gift shop. Today, Gina offers a large selection of perennials, native Texas plants, custom floral arrangements and gift baskets. She owes much of her success to Estelle and Glen. In fact, when Estelle passed away she left Gina a house, which Gina sold in order to pay for the new garden center building. A full circle of love between friends lives on in the beautiful blooms of Gina's garden. Stop by 1110 US Hwy. 84 W., visit www.goldthwaiteflorist.com or call 325-648-3704.

Pecans.com

Considered the "King and Queen of Pecans," DeWayne and Patty McCasland have a wonderful rags-to-riches story that is truly inspiring. They purchased a small parcel of land with pecan trees in 1972 and began harvesting their pecans literally on their hands and knees. Although they couldn't get a loan for what was considered a "risky business," they were able to borrow money on the cattle they owned. After one year in the pecan business, they were successful enough to pay for their mechanical harvesting equipment and have a little left over to start a new year. That humble beginning eventually led to them becoming overseers of the only pecan cooperative in the United States. Today, they manage more than 1000 acres of native pecans, supply 15 million pounds of locally harvested pecans to a major pecan sheller and own two retail stores.

Pecans.com 1, their first retail storefront, is located in San Angelo. Pecans.com 2 is located at the corner of W. Front and 4th St. in the original Southern Pacific Railroad siding. The building has served the community well, having originally housed a general feed store for more than 50 years. DeWayne and Patty turned the abandoned eye sore into a state-of-the-art custom shelling facility that not only supplies the two retail stores but services many Texas pecan growers. Both stores feature a large assortment of fresh-shelled pecans and pecan products like seasoned nuts, candy and gourmet pecan products, pies and cobblers; gift items like cookbooks and nutcrackers and even small equipment to do home cracking and shelling. You can even bring in pecans from your yard in the morning and pick up the shelled nuts that same afternoon. Order a catalog at www.pecans.com to check out corporate gift ideas and lucrative fundraising opportunities. Call 325-648-2200.

MILLS COUNTY HISTORICAL MUSEUM

The Mills County Historical Museum, 1119 Fisher St., was established during the bi-centennial in 1975 as a pictorial museum. The main part of the museum is housed in the historical Palmer Building, one of the first buildings built in 1893 in the newly formed railroad town of Goldthwaite. The town panicked when in 2000, a terrible fire broke out in buildings adjacent to the museum. Almost 100 citizens spontaneously showed up to empty the museum of all its historical content and everything was taken to surrounding homes and ranches for safekeeping until reopening in 2002. Today, there are 6,000 square feet of display space for exhibits that depict the history of the areas railroads and other notable landmarks like an old dentist office, drugstore, beauty shop, general store and one-room schoolhouse. The first car ever purchased in Mills County, a gorgeous 1906 Cadillac, greets visitors as they enter the museum. It's a beauty! For more information, call 325-648-6212.

The citizens of Goldthwaite are extremely excited about their one-of-a-kind interactive museum that will include the Texas Botanical Gardens & Native American Interpretive Center. Visitors will be able to "leap" far back in time—thousands of years ago—into the world of the ancient Americans who once roamed Central Texas. Walk through the "wikiup-shaped" entrance and watch the early natives as they use flat bedrock mortars to grind or mill plants or bake wild onion tubers in burned rock middens. Legacy Plaza, in Goldthwaite, will offer tremendous educational and hands-on learning opportunities for schools and universities, and the chance for visitors to understand the importance of these archeological finds and the history of the people who lived here 10,000 years ago. The gardens will feature native plants and indicate their advantage in central Texas landscapes, parks, yards, and ranches. To learn more about this state-of-the-art center and opening dates, call 325-648-3500 or visit www.legacyplaza.org.

Restaurants

Two of the things Machelle Baird loves most in life are cooking and serving people, and she gets the opportunity to do both very well as owner of the Texas Star Restaurant in Goldthwaite. The popular lunch stop, located inside the old Goldthwaite Florist at 1006 Fisher St., is known for its homemade Chicken Salad and original Ranch Potato Salad. Of course, everything is delicious and made fresh daily. One of our favorites is the "Krista," a ham and Swiss cheese sandwich served with raspberry jam on French toast. Just be sure to save room for a scrumptious dessert—everyone's favorite is the rich and gooey peanut butter pie. But wait, that's not all! Texas Star also offers catering, as well as a full line of custom-made jewelry and other gift items. Don't miss this chance to be truly treated like a Texas star! Call 325-451-7205.

Discover
San Saba & Lampasas

Pecan pie, pecan syrup, pecan candy, pecan salsas and sauces. If it can be made from pecans, you'll find it here in the "Pecan Capital of the World." Picturesque San Saba is a quaint town with a diverse variety of things to see and do and is a beautiful Hill Country paradise for hunters and fishermen. There is a delightful small historic downtown shopping district, a beautiful 18-hole golf course and the sparkling San Saba River to entertain visitors, so there is something for everyone to enjoy.

San Saba History (in a nutshell)

San Saba was named for its location on the San Saba River and became the county seat for San Saba County in 1856, but artifacts found during the last 75 years reveal that the area was thickly populated by prehistoric man many, many years before its settlement. Before the pioneers, the area was home to numerous Indian tribes, including the Comanches, Lipans, Cherokees, Wacos, Caddoes and Kickapoos. The name *San Saba* originated in 1755 when a Spaniard named Juan Antonio Bustillo y Zevallos, along with the Lipan Indians established a mission and presidio along the river on Holy Saturday (Santo Sabado). From that mission came the name for the city, the county and the river—San Saba. The first Anglo-Americans did not begin to move into the area until 1839, and the first community in the county was recorded in 1847.

Huge cattle drives began from Texas to Kansas in 1848. They brought with them prospectors looking for large areas of grazing land for their cattle. The wide-open ranges in San Saba County proved to be a popular place for cattlemen who filed on land and brought in thousands of heads of cattle. In fact, following the Civil War, trail driving became an important part of San Saba County's economy.

Pecan Capital of the World!

How does a tiny Texas town become known as the Pecan Capital of the World? Pecans have always been an abundant cash crop in the area since as early as 1857, and it is believed that some of the trees were growing here when Columbus discovered America. But San Saba's reputation for pecans took on a new importance during the early 1870s when an amateur horticulturist from England named Edmond E. Risien staged a pecan show to find the best pecan specimen. The winner was a light-colored, thin-shell pecan that was so good he bought the tree and land on which it stood. Risien planted the first commercial pecan nursery in San Saba County, setting out more than 600 trees with this nut as the original seed, then waited 12 to 14 years for the trees to bear. Then, by cross-pollination his trees produced popular varieties such as Onliwon, San Saba Improved, Western Shley and Squirrels Delight. Today, hundreds of thousands of pecan trees are planted throughout the verdant area, producing between two- and five-million pounds of pecans each season. Risien's great grandchildren continue in the pecan business with Millican Pecans, and it is in the heart of their orchard that the San Saba Mother Pecan Tree still stands. (They do not, however, allow public access to the tree.)

Pecan Capital Trade Day, which is sponsored by the city of San Saba, takes place on the first Saturday of each month, where vendors from across central Texas provide visitors with a wonderful selection of antiques and collectibles, home décor, art, jewelry and fresh produce.

Sites of the City

There's more than one famous tree in San Saba. Besides the famous Mother Pecan, the town is proud of their legendary

"*Wedding Oak*," which is located on China Creek Road. Also known as the Marriage Oak and the Matrimonial Oak, the enormous tree is known to have sheltered many marriage ceremonies during the 1900s. Legend says that before San Saba was settled, Indians stood under the tree to be wed and that the tradition was then adopted by the white settlers. The 400-year- old Wedding Oak remains a popular site and is listed in the book, "*Famous Trees of Texas*".

Historic downtown San Saba offers visitors a glimpse into its history with "A Walk *Along Wallace Street.*" The turn-of-the-century buildings have had many owners and gone through many renovations through the years, and each has a wonderful story to tell. As in most small Texas towns, the downtown is its own history book; so much care is taken to preserve these wonderful old buildings.

For a lazy day in San Saba, pack a picnic lunch and enjoy the serenity of Mill Pond Park, which was the site of the city's first waterworks. In 1875, Mr. Guy Risien built a rock and brush dam across Mill Creek for a hydraulic dam, and most of this dam still stands. He sold the waterworks to John Brown, who later built a gristmill on the site, and it is in that old gristmill that the city water system was housed. Mill Pond still provides water to the residents of San Saba. Today, the 71-acre Mill Pond Park has a spring-fed lake and a manmade swimming pool, with a waterfall that cascades over rocks, ferns and flowers. Seventy- million gallons of water bubble up from the natural springs to form the 15,000-square-foot pond. The waters flow under a bridge and throughout the beautiful park where you'll find picnic areas that are perfect for a wonderful day with the family. The park also houses baseball fields, tennis courts, a playground, basketball courts, and nature trails and is the location of the San Saba Civic Center and the San Saba County Museum.

Discover Lampasas

"Lampazos" was the name given to this charming little community by the Spanish Aquayo Expedition in 1721. It was a land of seven mineral springs that attracted tribes of Indians long before the white settlers began to claim the land. These springs also drew the first white man, Moses Hughes, who brought his wife to the area after hearing of their healing properties. First named Burleson, for the man who helped establish the town with a land grant, the town was eventually incorporated in 1883 as Lampasas. The mineral springs are still great attractions today; some with popular swimming holes and camping grounds.

Be sure to visit the historic Lampasas County Courthouse Square and the charming district that surrounds it. Read about the great stores we've discovered here and enjoy a wonderful day of exploring for antiques, jewelry, books and unusual gifts. And, check the dates you are visiting for fun parties and festivals during the year, especially the popular "Spring Ho Festival."

For additional information on San Saba, call the San Saba Chamber of Commerce at 325-372-5141 or visit www.sansabachamber.com.

Call 512-556-5172, 866-556-5172 or visit www.lampasaschamber.org for additional information on Lampasas.

San Saba / Lampasas Fairs Festivals & Fun

April
Annual Bloomin'Fest

June
Riata Roundup Rodeo

July
Spring Ho Festival

October
Herb Art Festival

November
Welcome Hunter's Day
The Best Little Fish Fry in Texas & Cake Auction

December
Christmas on the Square & Lighted Parade

Bed and Breakfasts, Cottages & Inns

Lancaster's
Pecan Grove
Bed & Breakfast

On a 600-acre Lampasas cattle ranch along the Lucy Creek, you'll find the perfect place for absolute peace and relaxation, a quiet get-away, or romantic weekend for two. Lancaster's Pecan Grove, 6415 CR 3420, is a charming limestone country cottage with a fireplace and fully furnished kitchen. Bring a fishing pole and enjoy fishing in the creek, or kick off your shoes and wade below the dam in complete privacy. You can hike the nature trails, enjoy the abundant wildflowers and get a chance to spot a wide variety of birds. In the evenings, you'll hear turkeys gobbling and the call of the whippoorwills. Owners Charles and Sue Lancaster purchased the ranch in 1977 and built the guest house for visiting friends and relatives. They now love sharing their beautiful little slice of Texas paradise with others, and you'll love Sue's yummy lemon pound cake! Visit www.lancasterpecangrove.net or call 512-556-2085.

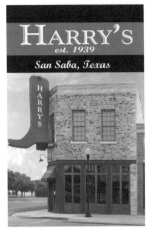

The giant "Harry's" cowboy boot over the front of the building welcomes visitors to not only one of the largest and most remarkable Western stores in Texas, but also into a part of San Saba's downtown history. Harry's, 403 E. Wallace St. at the intersection of Highways 16 and 190, is a landmark Western wear and boot store that covers almost the entire city block.

This success story began during San Saba's young days in 1907 when J. W. McConnell built two buildings—one as McConnell's Grocery and the other as the city's first men's clothing store. In 1939, Ike Shapiro purchased both buildings and opened what is still known today as Harry's, offering quality merchandise at competitive prices. In 1941, his son Harry joined the family business, and in 1970, he purchased the building next door, which had been The Corner Drug store for 60 years. Together, they grew Harry's into a strong Texas legacy.

Ike passed away in 1951 and Harry in 1982. The store was then purchased by two former employees, Lorena Terry and David Parker. Again, an additional next-door building was added and many renovations were made. Although the four turn-of-the-century buildings have had many owners, their character and history remain an integral part of the store's success.

Current owners Ken Jordan and Clay Nettleship have restored much of the buildings' original beauty, revealing wonderful native rock walls and lustrous hardwood floors. Their impressive inventory includes popular Western clothing lines for all ages, cowboy boots and hats in every color and size, hunting clothes and accessories, jeweled accessories and more. Harry's is truly an authentic Texas experience. Visit www.harrysboots.com or call 325-372-3636. *(Color photo featured in front section of book.)*

With everything from embroidery necessities and coffee pots to barbecue tongs and pasta bowls, Sisters' Country Store delivers exactly what its name suggests. Housed in a wonderful historical building with hardwood floors and interior brick walls, Sisters' displays kitchen gadgets, aromatic candles, craft and sewing supplies—everything you can imagine to make the kitchen the most exciting room in the house. Susie Nettleship opened Sisters' in 2006, and named it for her two adorable daughters, who she hopes one day will carry on her dream. The store is located at 410 E. Wallace St. in San Saba's downtown district. Susie's husband Clay designed the restoration of the handsome, historical building, showcasing the original walls and beautiful hardwood floors.

Display shelves showcase selections of unique dinnerware and cookware by names such as Cowboy Living, Emeril, Krups, KitchenAid and OGGI. You'll also find the ever-popular line of colorful Fiestaware, a great selection of both classic and current cookbooks and every kitchen gadget you can imagine. With outdoor living so popular now, you (and your husband) will appreciate the large selection of items for outdoor kitchens and grills. This is a store even the kiddos will love. It has one of the largest selections and highest quality toys in the Hill Country.

One of the wall plaques for sale says, "It Ain't Braggin' If It's True!" We're Braggin', but Sisters' is truly one of the most enjoyable places you'll ever shop. There is something for everyone. The customer service is charming, and you'll leave with something fabulous you didn't know you've always needed! Visit www.sisterscountrystore.net to see the large selection of items, or call 325-372-5030.

(Color photo featured in front section of book.)

Realtors

 GENE STEWART REAL ESTATE

Since 1988

Folks are finally discovering San Saba— one of the most picturesque regions in the heart of the Lone Star State. Ranches and farms dot the rugged hills and rolling plains, hunting and fishing opportunities abound, and the town is a small, friendly community. No one knows this area better than Gene and Sylvia Stewart. With Gene's Agri-Business degree, lifetime of ranching know-how, love for the great outdoors, and 31 years of experience, he is an expert in the farm and ranch real estate business. Gene says, "We enjoy what we do, and take time to understand our customers' needs and wants. Plus it doesn't hurt that we are located in one of the most scenic areas in Texas. That is just an extra blessing from God!" Let Gene and Sylvia help you find your lovely Hill Country home. Stop by 1307 W. Wallace St., or visit www.GeneStewartRealEstate.com, to browse through the many properties for sale. Call 325-372-5082 or 888-384-5777.

Restaurants & Drive-Ins

 Elvis liked it here, and you will too! Featured on The Food Channel's *Best Of* television series, this 60-year-old family-owned restaurant will put a smile on your face with its classic drive-in food. The managerial team of Mike Green, Kenny Murray, Sharon Carrigan and David Wiggins still produce burgers, fries, malts and shakes just like they made them in the 50s. The King of Rock 'n' Roll loved bacon on his burgers. You might like the ham-and-cheese stuffed Cordon Bleu burger. For smaller appetites order the mini-sized burger or try a grilled chicken salad. For more information, call 512-556-6269 or visit 201 N. Key Ave. in Lampasas. Check out Storm's other locations at www.stormsrestaurants.com.

Index

Cross Reference

Antiques

A Step Back'n Time - 83
Alley Cats - 143
Antique Revival - 53
Barton & Beane - 142
Between Friends - 163, 172
Brazos Moon - 14
Cottage Antiques - 164
Country Jar Mall - 214
Homestead House - 206
J & Co. - 148
Ladybug Jungle - 171
Main Street Mercantile - 82
MSC Forsyth - 186
Plan it Home - 129
Serendipity - 161
The Apothecary - 232
The Broad Street Mall - 162
The Cottage - 107
The Curious Wren - 122
The Eloia - 209
The Mustard Seed - 130
Two 0 Five - 141
Uniques & Antiques - 164
Vintage Charm - 163

Artists/Art Galleries/Framing/
   Photography

Artèfactz - 15
Beads on the Vine - 70
Bermuda Gold & Silver - 69
Boutique Ginny - 198
Common Scents - 208
Cowboy Up - 213
D&S Premier - 188
Dragonfly Art Studio - 165
Fancy This - 66
Griffith Fine Art - 221
Holy Grounds - 65
J. Wayne Stark Galleries - 185
Mineola League of the Arts - 165
MSC Forsyth - 186
MudCreek Pottery - 207
Painting with a Twist - 55
Plan it Home - 129
Salado Arts Workshop - 221

Sofi's - 230
Something Special - 91
Southern Grace - 184
The Apothecary - 232
The Frame Gallery - 189
The Village - 200
Timeless Designs - 199
U paint·it - 188
Uniques & Antiques - 164
Weatherford Art Association - 84

Attractions/Entertainment

Adelea's on Main - 235
Alexander's Distillery - 234
Baymont Inn & Suites - 131
Beads on the Vine - 70
Calvert Historical Foundation - 210
Catalena Hatters - 193
Chandor Gardens - 85
Clark Gardens - 86
Depot Museum - 133
Doss Heritage and Culture Center - 87
East Texas Oil Museum - 145
Granbury Opera House - 17
Granbury Resort Conference Center - 18
Grapevine Opry - 54
Henderson Civic Center - 135
Hidden Oaks - 18
Howard-Dickinson House - 133
Kitchens - 175
Lake Country Playhouse - 166
Line Camp Steakhouse - 39
London Museum - 132
Mills County Historical Museum - 251
Mineola Civic Center - 167
Mineola League of the Arts - 165
MoJoe's - 125
MSC OPAS - 187
Painting with a Twist - 55
Panola County Historical - 108
Rangerette Showcase Museum - 144
Salado Arts Workshop - 221
Salado Creek Winery - 237
Salado Silver Spur Theater - 222
Texas Botanical Gardens - 252
Texas Star Feline Preservation - 210

The Back Porch - 154
The Eloia - 209
The Village - 200
The Vineyards - 59
The Windmill Farm - 19
U paint·it - 188
Wagon Yard - 29
Weatherford Art Association - 84
Wooden Spoon - 215

Bakeries
MainStreet Bistro - 71
Patty Cakes Bakery - 73
Roy T's - 235
The Vineyard at Florence - 238
The Wedding Connection - 23
Zamykal - 211

Bed & Breakfasts/Cabins/Cottages
Abigaile's Treehouse - 191
Angel's Nest - 89
Babe's & Min's Cottages - 21
Baines House - 225
Comfort Suites - 151
Fisher Street - 246
Garden Manor - 56
Granbury Gardens - 20
Granbury Log Cabins - 20
Inn on Lake Granbury - 36
Inn on the Creek - 224
Lancaster's Pecan Grove - 258
Munzesheimer Manor - 168
Parish House - 212
Pine Tree - 169
Red Barn Hideaway - 226
Rudder Jessup B&B - 190
StoneCreek Settlement – 223, 236
The Clary House - 191
The Historic Nutt House - 37
The Rose Garden Cottage - 88
The Vineyard at Florence - 238
The Vineyards - 59
The Windmill Farm - 19

Books
Books on the Square - 22
Holy Grounds - 65
Sisters' - 260

Bridal/Weddings
Angel's Nest - 89
Beauty Sense - 110
Bermuda Gold & Silver - 69
Chandor Gardens - 85
Clark Gardens - 86
Doss Heritage and Culture Center - 87
Expressions - 147
Garden Manor – 56
Granbury Gardens - 20
Granbury Resort Conference Center - 18
Howard-Dickinson House - 133
Inn on Lake Granbury - 36
Inn on the Creek - 224
LaSalle Hotel - 196
Main Street Flowers & More - 150
MainStreet Bistro - 71
Mineola Civic Center - 167
Munzesheimer Manor - 168
Parish House - 212
Pearl Street Station - 38
Rafter B Ranch House - 245
Renata Salon & Day Spa - 74
StoneCreek Settlement - 223, 236
Texas Star - 253
The Clary House - 191
The Hobby Horse - 111
The Jeweler's Workshop - 16
The Vineyard at Florence - 238
The Wedding Connection - 23

Camping/RVing
Cowboy MarketPlace - 30
Mineola RV Park - 170
Texas Star Feline Preservation - 210
The Vineyards - 59

Catering
Adelea's on Main - 235
Babe's - 40
Buck's Pizza - 114
Butch's Brick Pit BBQ - 215
Claudia's - 124
MainStreet Bistro – 71
Mesquite Pit - 98
Nanny Goat's - 152
Patty Cakes Bakery - 73

Pearl Street Station - 38
Tarbutton - 125
Texas Star - 253
Weatherford Downtown Café - 99
Weinberger's Deli - 72

Children's
Artèfactz - 15
Back to Yesterday - 95
Books on the Square - 22
Coyote Cowboy - 63
Depot Museum - 133
Heart to Heart - 146
Hidden Oaks - 18
J & Co. - 148
Kid Kraze - 123
Let's Pretend - 58
London Museum - 132
MudCreek Pottery - 207
Mulberry Bush - 109
Salado Arts Workshop - 221
Sisters' - 260
Splendors - 233
The Curious Wren - 122
U paint·it - 188
Willow Cottage - 61

Coffee
Charlotte's - 229
Foxx III Salon - 134
Holy Grounds - 65
MoJoe's - 125
Roy T's - 235
The Pan Handle - 32
Zamykal - 211

Condominiums/Resorts/Rentals
Comfort Suites - 151
Pine Tree - 169
Plantation Inn - 37

Cosmetics/Health & Beauty
   Products
Beauty Sense - 110
Christy's - 227
Debonair Salon Spa - 101
Ken Turner Pharmacy - 113
McMahan Pharmacy - 248

St. Helen's - 35
The Apothecary - 232

Fashion/Accessories
A Step Back'n Time - 83
Ashlins, Ltd. - 67
Azure Alley - 60
B.J. Taylor & Co. - 126
Beauty Sense - 110
Bella Rosa - 26
Bermuda Gold & Silver - 69
Boutique Ginny - 198
Cactus Flower - 27
Calamity Jane's - 149
Catalena Hatters - 193
Christy's - 227
Closet Treasures - 61
Common Scents - 208
Copper Falls & Co. - 112
Cowboy Up - 213
Coyote Cowboy - 63
Foxx III Salon - 134
Harry's - 259
Head 2 Toe - 43
Heart to Heart - 146
Hearthstone Gallery - 127
J & Co. - 148
Jean's Crossing - 24
Jim·n·I - 192
Ken Turner Pharmacy - 113
Kid Kraze - 123
Ladybug Jungle - 171
Old Bryan Marketplace - 194
Ooh La La - 62
Pizazz - 27
Scentimentals - 92
Side by Side - 228
Sofi's - 230
Something Special - 91
Southern Grace - 184
St. Helen's - 35
Stuff~N~Nonsense - 25
The Clothes Horse - 25
The Jeweler's Workshop - 16
The Jewelry & Coin Exchange - 197
The Mustard Seed - 130
Timeless Designs - 199
Truly Trendy - 90

Western Heritage - 95
Witt's End - 192

Florists
Donovan's - 130
Homestead House - 206
Live Oak Florist - 249
Main Street Flowers & More - 150
The Wedding Connection - 23
Tricia Barksdale Designs - 195

Furniture
A Step Back'n Time - 83
Accents II - 31
Almost Heaven - 28
Barton & Beane - 142
Bella Rosa - 26
Cottage Antiques - 164
Cowboy MarketPlace - 30
Cowboy Up - 213
D & S Premier - 188
Dakota's Kabin - 33
GW Upholstery & Rafter W Furniture
  - 247
Homestead House - 206
Lane's - 30
Serendipity - 161
Side by Side - 228
Taylors - 231
The Broad Street Mall - 162
The Howling Wolff - 227, 230
Two 0 Five - 141
Uniques & Antiques - 164
Vintage Charm - 163
Wagon Yard - 29
Western Heritage - 95

Gardens/Nurseries
Almost Heaven - 28
Chandor Gardens - 85
Clark Gardens - 86
Country Jar Mall - 214
Donovan's - 130
Dragonfly Art Studio - 165
Fancy This - 66
Jordan's Plant Farm - 128
Live Oak Florist - 249
Splendors - 233

Texas Botanical Gardens - 252
The Copper Pumpkin - 93

Gifts/Home Décor
Accents II - 31
Alley Cats - 143
Almost Heaven - 28
Ambrosia Tea Room - 234
Artèfactz - 15
Ashlins, Ltd. - 67
B.J. Taylor & Co. - 126
Back to Yesterday - 95
Barton & Beane - 142
Beauty Sense - 110
Bella Rosa - 26
Between Friends - 163, 172
Books on the Square - 22
Brazos Moon - 14
British Emporium - 64
Cactus Flower - 27
Calamity Jane's - 149
Catalena Hatters - 193
Charlotte's - 229
Common Scents - 208
Copper Falls & Co. - 112
Cottage Antiques - 164
Country Jar Mall - 214
Cowboy MarketPlace - 30
Cowboy Up - 213
D&S Premier - 188
Dakota's Kabin - 33
Debonair Salon - 101
Donovan's - 130
Downtown Store - 33
Dragonfly Art Studio - 165
Expressions - 147
Fancy This - 66
Foxx III Salon - 134
Griffith Fine Art - 221
Head 2 Toe - 43
Heart to Heart - 146
Hearthstone Gallery - 127
Heritage House - 94
Holy Grounds - 65
Homestead House - 206
J & Co. - 148
Jean's Crossing - 24
Jim·n·i - 192

Jordan's Plant Farm - 128
Ken Turner Pharmacy - 113
Kid Kraze - 123
Kitchens - 175
Lane's - 30
Main Street Mercantile - 82
McMahan Pharmacy - 248
MudCreek Pottery - 207
Mulberry Bush - 109
Off the Vine - 75
Old Bryan Marketplace - 194
Ooh La La - 62
Pamela & Co. - 34
Pandamonium - 68
Pizazz - 27
Salado Creek Winery - 237
Scentimentals - 92
Side by Side - 228
Sisters' - 260
Sofi's - 230
Southern Grace - 184
Splendors - 233
St. Helen's - 35
Stuff~N~Nonsense - 25
Taylors - 231
Texas Star - 253
The Broad Street Mall - 162
The Copper Pumpkin - 93
The Curious Wren - 122
The Frame Gallery - 189
The Hobby Horse - 111
The Howling Wolff - 227, 230
The Mustard Seed - 130
The Pan Handle - 32
Timeless Designs - 199
Tricia Barksdale - 195
Two 0 Five - 141
U paint·it - 188
Uniques & Antiques - 164
Vintage Charm - 163
Wagon Yard - 29
Weatherford Art Association - 84
Western Heritage - 95
Willow Cottage - 61

Golf
Hidden Oaks - 18

Gourmet/Specialty Foods
Between Friends - 163, 172
British Emporium - 64
Butch's Brick Pit - 215
Country Jar Mall - 214
Dakota's Kabin - 33
Downtown Store - 33
J & Co. - 148
Lee's Old Country Store - 173
Live Oak Florist - 249
Pamela & Co. - 34
Patty Cakes Bakery - 73
Pecans.com - 250
Sisters' - 260
Splendors - 233
The Pan Handle - 32
Timeless Designs - 199
Weinberger's Deli - 72
Willow Cottage - 61
Zamykal - 211

Hotels/Inns
Abigaile's Treehouse - 191
Baines House - 225
Baymont Inn & Suites - 131
Comfort Suites - 151
Fisher Street - 246
Garden Manor - 56
Inn on the Creek - 224
LaQuinta Inns & Suites - 96
LaSalle Hotel - 196
Pine Tree - 169
Plantation Inn - 37
Rafter B Ranch House - 245
Residence Inn Marriott - 57
The Clary House - 191
The Historic Nutt House - 37
Weatherford Lodgings - 97

Ice Cream Parlors
Roy T's - 235
Yesterday's - 100

Interior Décor/Designs
Accents II - 31
Almost Heaven - 28
Ashlins, Ltd. - 67
Back to Yesterday - 95

Barton & Beane - 142
Cactus Flower - 27
Cowboy MarketPlace - 30
Cowboy Up - 213
D & S Premier - 188
Donovan's - 130
Expressions - 147
GW Upholstery & Rafter W Furniture - 247
Heritage House - 94
Homestead House - 206
Lane's - 30
Pandamonium - 68
Plan it Home - 129
Taylors - 231
The Howling Wolff - 227, 230
Tricia Barksdale - 195
Two 0 Five - 141
Wagon Yard - 29
Western Heritage - 95

Jewelry
Artèfactz - 15
Azure Alley - 60
B.J. Taylor & Co. - 126
Back to Yesterday - 95
Barton & Beane - 142
Beads on the Vine - 70
Bermuda Gold & Silver - 69
Boutique Ginny - 198
Brazos Moon - 14
Cactus Flower - 27
Charlotte's - 229
Christy's - 227
Closet Treasures - 61
Common Scents - 208
Copper Falls & Co. - 112
Cowboy MarketPlace - 30
Cowboy Up - 213
Griffith Fine Art - 221
Heart to Heart - 146
Heritage House - 94
Holy Grounds - 65
Jean's Crossing - 24
Jim·n·i - 192
Ken Turner Pharmacy - 113
Kid Kraze - 123
Ladybug Jungle - 171

Main Street Flowers & More - 150
Pamela & Co. - 34
Pizazz - 27
Plan it Home - 129
Scentimentals - 92
Something Special - 91
Southern Grace - 184
St. Helen's - 35
Stuff~N~Nonsense - 25
Texas Star - 253
The Apothecary - 232
The Broad Street Mall - 162
The Clothes Horse - 25
The Curious Wren - 122
The Hobby Horse - 111
The Howling Wolff - 227, 230
The Jeweler's Workshop - 16
The Jewelry & Coin Exchange - 197
The Mustard Seed - 130
Timeless Designs - 199
Truly Trendy - 90
Vintage Charm - 163
Willow Cottage - 61
Witt's End - 192

Museums
Depot Museum - 133
Doss Heritage and Culture Center - 87
East Texas Oil Museum - 145
Howard-Dickinson House - 133
J. Wayne Stark Galleries - 185
London Museum - 132
Mills County Historical Museum - 251
Panola County Historical - 108
Rangerette Showcase Museum - 144

Orchards/Produce
Pecans.com - 250

Pampered Pets
J & Co. - 148

Quilts/Needlework/Stitchery
Cottage Antiques - 164
Houston St. Mercantile - 45
Main Street Mercantile - 82
Mineola League of the Arts - 165

Line Camp Steakhouse - 39
London Museum - 132
MainStreet Bistro - 71
Mesquite Pit - 98
Mills County Historical Museum - 251
Mineola Civic Center - 167
Mineola League of the Arts - 165
MoJoe's - 125
MSC OPAS - 187
MudCreek Pottery - 207
Munzesheimer Manor - 168
Nanny Goat's - 152
Off the Vine - 75
Old Bryan Marketplace - 194
OldWest Café - 72
Painting with a Twist - 55
Panola County Historical - 108
Parish House - 212
Patty Cakes Bakery - 73
Pearl Street Station - 38
Plantation Inn - 37
Rafter B Ranch House - 245
Rangerette Showcase Museum - 144
Red Barn Hideaway - 226
Renata Salon & Day Spa - 74
Residence Inn Marriott - 57
Rudder Jessup B&B - 190
Salado Arts Workshop - 221
Salado Silver Spur Theater - 222
StoneCreek Settlement - 223, 236
Storm's - 262
Texas Botanical Gardens - 252
Texas Star - 253
Texas Star Feline Preservation - 210
The Back Porch - 154
The Clary House - 191
The Eloia - 209
The Historic Nutt House - 37
The Hobby Horse - 111
The Rose Garden Cottage - 88
The Windmill Farm - 19
U paint·it - 188
Weatherford Downtown Café - 99
Weinberger's Deli - 72
Willow Cottage - 61
Wooden Spoon - 215
Zamykal - 211

Specialty Shops
Alley Cats - 143
B.J. Taylor & Co. - 126
Bella Rosa - 26
Between Friends - 163, 172
Boutique Ginny - 198
Brazos Moon - 14
British Emporium - 64
Calamity Jane's - 149
Catalena Hatters - 193
Closet Treasures - 61
Copper Falls & Co. - 112
Coyote Cowboy - 63
D & S Premier - 188
Dakota's Kabin - 33
Donovan's - 130
Doug's Sports House - 44
Downtown Store - 33
Dragonfly Art Studio - 165
Fancy This - 66
GW Upholstery & Rafter W Furniture
 - 247
Harry's - 259
Heart to Heart - 146
Holy Grounds - 65
Houston St. Mercantile - 45
Jordan's Plant Farm - 128
Ken Turner Pharmacy - 113
Lee's Old Country Store - 173
Main Street Flowers & More - 150
McMahan Pharmacy - 248
Mulberry Bush - 109
Off the Vine - 75
Ooh La La - 62
Pamela & Co. - 34
Pecans.com - 250
Plan it Home - 129
Pro-Tek Guns - 155
Salado Creek Winery - 237
Serendipity - 161
Side by Side - 228
Sisters' - 260
Sofi's - 230
Something Special - 91
St. Helen's - 35
The Clothes Horse - 25
The Copper Pumpkin - 93
The Curious Wren - 122

Dear Adventurer,

If you are reading this book chances are you are an 'Adventurer.' An 'Adventurer' is a person with a sense of adventure and a curiosity for new and exciting places, people and experiences—both long and short distances. All of the Lady's Day Out books appeal to that sense of adventure and cater to the natural curiosity in all of us.

A Lady's Day Out, Inc., would like to share this gift of the perfect combination between work and travel with our loyal following of readers.

In an effort to expand our coverage area we are looking for adventurous travelers who would like to help us find the greatest places to include in our upcoming editions of A Lady's Day Out. This is a wonderful opportunity to travel and explore some of the best destination cities in the United States.

If you would like more information, we would love to hear from you. You may call A Lady's Day Out, Inc. at 1-888-860-ALDO (2536) or e-mail us at info@ALadysDayOut.com or visit us at www. ALadysDayOut.com.

Best wishes and keep on exploring, from all of us at A Lady's Day Out, Inc.

Dear Entrepreneur,

If you would like to be a business partner or owner of A Lady's Day Out, Inc., please call so we can chat. After many years of traveling and exploring, the time to pass the torch is approaching. For just the right person or group, we will be considering offers to carry on the Legacy that Paula Ramsey has trusted to our care. Call 1-888-860-ALDO (2536) or 817-236-5250 if you are interested.

Thank you,
Jennifer Ramsey

A Lady's Day Out
Giveaway Entry Form

Have five of the businesses featured in this book sign your entry form and you are eligible to win one of the following: weekend-get-away at a bed and breakfast, dinner gift certificates, shopping spree gift certificates or $250 cash.

1. _____
   (NAME OF BUSINESS)   (SIGNATURE)

2. _____
   (NAME OF BUSINESS)   (SIGNATURE)

3. _____
   (NAME OF BUSINESS)   (SIGNATURE)

4. _____
   (NAME OF BUSINESS)   (SIGNATURE)

5. _____
   (NAME OF BUSINESS)   (SIGNATURE)

NAME: _____

ADDRESS: _____

CITY: _____ STATE: _____ ZIP: _____

PHONE#: _____ E – MAIL: _____

Where did you purchase book? _____

Other towns or businesses you feel should be incorporated in our next book.

_____

_____

No purchase necessary. Winners will be determined by random drawing from all complete entries received. Winners will be notified by phone and/or mail.

Mail To:
A Lady's Day Out, Inc.
PO Box 79608
Fort Worth, Tx 76179-0608

Fax To: 817-236-0033
Phone: 817-236-5250
www.ALadysDayOut.com
info@ALadysDayOut.com

NOTES

NOTES

NOTES

NOTES